NORTHWEST
W I N E
COMPANION

NORTHWEST
WINE
COMPANION

Ted Jordan Meredith

Nexus Press
Kirkland, Washington

Library of Congress Catalog Card Number: 88-60743
ISBN 0-936666-04-8

Additional copies of this book may be obtained by
sending $8.95 plus $1.00 for shipping to:

Nexus Press
P.O. Box 911
Kirkland, WA 98083

(Washington residents please add $.72 sales tax.)

Bookseller rates available on request.

Printed in the United States of America.

About the Author

Ted Jordan Meredith has been writing about the wines of America's Northwest in books, and in articles for national and regional publications, since 1974. Other wine books by Meredith include *Northwest Wine*, *The Wines and Wineries of America's Northwest*, and co-authorship of *A Dictionary of American Wines*, published by William Morrow, New York.

Meredith's works are widely regarded as the authoritative references on the wines of America's Northwest. Recently, for his contributions to wine literature, Meredith was invited to join the prestigious International Authors and Writers Who's Who in Cambridge, England.

Born in Montana, now a resident of Washington, Meredith holds a bachelor's degree in Sociology and a master's degree in Philosophy. He is a member of the Society of Wine Educators, the Enological Society of the Pacific Northwest, Washington Wine Writers, and various other industry and professional organizations.

In the circle, the beginning and the end are the same. Into the same rivers we step—and do not step.

Heraclitus
6th Century B.C.

Contents

We Can't Drink Gold— We Are Condemned to Freedom

W e can't drink gold. We cannot drink gold medals, or silver medals, or bronze medals. We can't drink numbers, or points, or stars.

We American winedrinkers seem to suffer a human affliction more severely than our European wine drinking counterparts from across the pond. Maybe it is our relative newness to wine drinking. Maybe it grows out of an exaggerated need to measure all things and reduce all things to objective absolutes—a need, even, to quantify esthetics.

Whatever the cause or reason, it is hard for us to decide, on our own, that we like a wine. We somehow feel the need to have someone tell us what we should like, to tell us what our choices should be, to affirm prospectively that we are cor- rect, to make us secure that we are right in what we like, to take away our freedom to choose and decide and enjoy—as if it were not we ourselves who surrender that freedom when we surrender our enjoyment and judgment to the granters of medals and the assigners of points.

It is not that medals and awards and competitions are wrong. They are not. They can be quite useful to us if we do not take them as absolute gospel. If we know who has evaluated the wines, know something of their biases, competency, likes and dislikes, we can properly regard the tasting results as suggestions for us.

I used to dread the results of competitions. If there were wines that I was thinking of buying or thought would be good but had not yet gotten around to trying, I would anxiously hope they would not win gold medals. A few years ago, when there were fewer competitions, a gold medal meant the wines would be instantly sold out or on limited allocation. Wine shop shelves were ravaged by desperate people armed with lists of gold medal dogma.

Wine merchants who cared nothing for Northwest wines and knew nothing of them would suddenly advertise lists of gold medal wines—an expedient circumvention of knowledge, understanding, enjoyment, and caring.

I got so I hated to buy wines that won gold medals. Inevitably, the wine merchant or salesperson would mention that the wine won a gold medal. I finally took to saying, to puzzled looks, "I know, but I liked it anyway."

❦   ❦   ❦   ❦   ❦

I have participated in formal tastings and competitions in the past. I will continue to do so in the future. There is much inherent goodness in them, for the wine industry and for us as consumers. Competitions raise our awareness and stimulate our interest in fine wine. They bring more people into our community of enjoyers-of-fine-wine. Competitions stimulate (or should stimulate) the quest for better quality wine. Today, fewer blatantly defective wines are made and entered into competitions.

It is easy for us to accept the judgment of others who we think must surely be more knowledgeable. The results of judgings, we think, must surely be quite objective.

Hopefully, more often than not, the wines that do well in competitions are deserving wines. And hopefully, more often than not, deserving wines do not go without adequate recognition. But this is not always so. It is an often repeated phrase, among winemakers and judges alike, that competitions "are a crapshoot." There are many reasons why judging results are less than wholly objective and absolute. Let's look at a few of them.

❦ ❦ ❦ ❦ ❦

Regional Judges

Judges from within the winegrowing region may be very familiar with the region's wines and wine styles. What others from outside the region or with more eclectic palates might consider an odd and uncharacteristic flavor, a regional judge might regard as a positive and unique character that sets the wines of the region above and apart from wines that do not possess the character. In some cases, the regional judge will fail to recognize and acknowledge inherent regional weaknesses. And whether Bordeaux, Burgundy, California, Washington, Oregon, or Idaho, every region has them.

Non-Regional Judges

Non-regional judges may have little familiarity or understanding of the wines of the region. What are the implications of a particular flavor? What will evolve from this flavor as the wine ages? If the wine is an unusual variety, what should it taste like and in what context should one place it?

These shortcomings are minimized if the judge has an eclectic palate, but if the judge comes from another winegrowing region and is most familiar with the wines of that region, the judge will tend to evaluate wines in accordance with the tastes and expectations of the wines of his native region, and rate most highly, wines that are not necessarily the best, but which most closely emulate the familiar wines of his native region.

Wine Writer Judges

Wine writers, Sommeliers, wine merchants, and restauranteurs encompass the worst and the best of the wine judging spectrum. As a category, they tend to overlook or be more tolerant of technical flaws in wine, including flaws that may become increasingly problematic if a wine is cellared.

Some in this category know startlingly little about wine. At the other end of the spectrum, perhaps exampled by the British Masters of Wine, are those who possess exceptional depth and breath of formal knowledge, as well as highly experienced, eclectic palates.

Winemaker Judges

Winemakers, particularly those who have had formal training in enology, tend to be highly attuned to technical flaws. Their job requires them to detect potential problems at the earliest possible instant. A winemaker judge will tend to severely downgrade a wine with any evidence of a technical flaw. A wonderful tasting wine with a minor technical flaw might be rated very highly by other judges and relegated to the dump bucket by a winemaker judge.

Winemakers have a stylistic agenda. The style of wine they make is usually the style they like best. There is, thus, a natural tendency to give higher ratings to wines that are most like their own. If a winemaker judge is from another region with a different regional style, the potential bias becomes even more onerous.

Unqualified Judges

Sometimes judges are chosen not for their competence, but because their occupational title or position suggests they would be knowledgeable about wine. I once had a casual conversation with a fellow judge who had just recently started work with a wine distributor. Except for wine coolers and White Zinfandel, the judge had little experience, love, or understanding of wine.

Impaired Judges

Because of a cold, illness, emotional distress, or other reasons, a judge's acuity may be diminished. Because of a sense of obligation, if nothing else, there is a tendency to persevere rather than to withdraw from the judging.

I was a judge at one competition where one of the judges was recovering from the flu. Another (myself) developed a severe headache during a tasting of a flight of wines of a variety he did not particularly care for (another bias). I should have withdrawn from that flight of wines. I did not. I hope my assessments were not too far from the mark.

Dominant Judges

Most judgings, with good reason, include a discussion of which wines (their identity still unknown) should be awarded medals. Because of status or oratory skills, one judge may dominate the others. Others may tend to fall in line, so as not to admit they had not tasted or perceived or understood some quality—or to decide that, after all, they had indeed perceived that quality and its implications. The judging thus becomes a panel of one. If that one has a particular bias, the judging panel and the judging results take on that bias.

Politics and Publicity

Judges are sometimes chosen not for their ability to judge well, but for their potential for publicizing the event, or for appearance of legitimacy and importance they might bring to the event, or because they have a bias which agrees with the bias of the competition organizers, or for any number of other reasons not necessarily related to their judging abilities.

Personal Bias

All of us have bias's and personal agendas. Judges are no different. They may tend to rate late harvest Rieslings higher or lower than Cabernets, for example, or fresh, fruity, crisply acidic Chardonnays higher or lower than richer, fuller, more traditionally styled Chardonnays. A judge may recognize that a wine is from a particular winery and tend to rate the wine based on the likes or dislikes of the winery rather than the wine.

We all have preferences and opinions—at least I certainly do. The esthetics of wine is necessarily subjective. The notion that a tasting or judging of wine can be wholly objective and forever absolute is nonsense.

Bias of Expectation

Expectations inevitably interject bias. All reputable judgings and formal tastings evaluate wines blind, i.e., without knowing their identity, but the type of wine is generally known. Expectations for a category of wines can lead to a positive or negative bias for all the wines of the group.

At one judging, flights of wines were separated by vintage. One of the vintages was widely publicized and highly regarded. One wine was inadvertently mislabeled and entered twice, once in the highly regarded vintage category, and once as its true vintage. The wine, judged as a wine from the highly regarded vintage, was awarded a gold medal. When it was judged as a wine from a less highly regarded vintage, it "earned" no gold, and was ranked considerably less well. After all, wines from the more highly regarded vintage should be better shouldn't they? Or at least, so goes the bias of expectation.

Deficient Judging Criteria

All rating scales and point systems have deficiencies. The traditional U. C. Davis twenty point system, for example, is at its best when applied to utilitarian, commercial grade wines. Much of the Davis point system is devoted to weeding out wines with technical flaws. There is relatively little focus on the esthetic complexities of premium wine.

17

Deficient judging criteria may take other forms. Instructions to judges may be flawed. I judged at one event, for example, where we were told to "judge the wines as they taste now, not on their potential." This is an absurd criteria, particularly for red wines. Great red wines are frequently hard and unfriendly in their youth, a necessity for the greatness that will come from aging them. Such a criteria would relegate the world's greatest red wines to the heap of also-rans. Harmless Beaujolais Nouveau would forever be king.

Stand-Out Wines versus Outstanding Wines

Tasting many wines quickly fatigues the palate and impairs the ability to distinguish quality and difference. A wine that is pleasant but clearly stands out from the rest may readily garner favorable attention and be rated highly. The same wine, if evaluated the way we drink wine for pleasure, with food over a relatively lengthy period of time, might seem over obvious in character, simplistic, and wearing on the palate, and perhaps even a bit odd. A wine with a multitude of subtle complexities would fair much better.

The Crapshoot Factor

Winemakers and judges freely admit that wine judgings are something of a crapshoot. At an important judging one year, one winery won a gold medal and a rare special distinction award that is granted only rarely. Several years later, the winemaker, not noted for self-aggrandizement or hyperbole, believed he had made a wine that was even superior to his earlier, much awarded wine. Others agreed with his assessment.

He entered the wine in the same judging. The wine not only failed to win the special award or a gold medal—it won no medal at all. "It's too bad," commented one knowledgeable wine merchant, "but it's great for us. It gives us a great wine we can recommend to our customers, and it won't sell out everywhere in a frenzy for a gold medal wine."

❦   ❦   ❦   ❦   ❦

Competitions and judgings are not inherently onerous, nor are they inherently meaningless. The results of formal tastings and judgings are simply a collective opinion. If we regard the results as absolute dogma, then it is we who are to blame for their misuse. We are to blame when we surrender our freedom of judgment and enjoyment. No one can be our surrogate. No one can enjoy for us.

If it is true what the French existentialist philosopher, Jean-Paul Sartre, said, that we are condemned to freedom, then, at least in food and wine, this condemnation is truly a joyous one. Let us fully accept our freedom to think, to evaluate, to understand, to judge, and, above all, to enjoy.

Oregon Pinot Noir— the Path to Greatness

If Oregon Pinot Noir is so great, why do so many quickly turn brown with age? Why have most failed to develop the complex character associated with great wines, particularly, great Pinot Noir? Why do wines that tasted so rich and fruity when they were first released, later taste flat, soft, and dull, with a cloying, almost sweetish character? Does Oregon really produce great Pinot Noir?

Emphatically, yes! Today's Oregon Pinot Noir is arguably the Northwest's finest wine. But today's Oregon Pinot Noir is quite different than most that were produced in earlier years. There are several interrelated reasons for the strides in quality. We will look at others later, but a major reason is higher total acidity, and, most importantly, lower pH in today's Oregon Pinot Noirs.

pH is correlated closely, but not exactly, with total acidity. In general, higher acidity means lower pH. The entries for total acidity and pH in the encyclopedia section of this book offer a more detailed explanation.

In the early years of the modern Oregon wine industry, facing skeptics who said that the western Oregon climate was too cool and wet to grow good wine grapes, most Oregon winegrowers focused their attention on getting grapes with high sugars. Acidity was only a concern if it seemed too high in cool years, or if a successful malolactic fermentation was a problem. Chaptalization, the addition of sugar to the grape must, was avoided, as if in fear it would somehow prove the skeptics right. The ideal became very ripe grapes with very high sugars and low acids. pH was not a topic of interest.

Today, for the majority of Oregon winegrowers, the focus is reversed. It is now understood that grape ripeness is not achieved at a given sugar level. In cooler climates, grapes become physiologically ripe at lower sugars. Achieving maximum sugar at all cost is no longer the emphasis.

Now, grapes are picked more according to physiological ripeness, acid, and pH, rather than sugars. If necessary, acid is added to the juice. Chaptalization is employed in cool years. The ideal, now, is ripe, but not overripe grapes, with balanced acid, sugar, and pH. This translates into balanced wines with lower pH and far better aging potential than in the past.

pH measurements of some 50 Oregon Pinot Noirs, from 1975 through 1985, illustrate the important trend toward lower pH levels (and higher acidity) in Oregon Pinot Noir. Analysis of the wines was made possible by Dr. Bruce Watson, a member of the research faculty at the University of Washington

Botany Department, who assayed the samples and provided technical advice and assistance.

The results illustrate a clear trend. Oregon Pinot Noirs from the vintages prior to 1980 measured an average pH of 3.84. For the vintages in the 1980s, the average pH was 3.64. For 1978 and 1979, two very warm vintages, average pH measurements were 3.91 and 3.92 respectively. The 1978 pH range was the most extreme. One wine from the 1978 vintage measured an extraordinarily high pH of 4.31. In contrast, 1983 and 1985, two other, more recent, very warm vintages, had much lower pHs of 3.70 and 3.60 respectively.

Fine French Burgundies age superbly, developing incredibly complex flavors and scents over a long life in the cellar. How do their pH measurements compare? An ad hoc selection of French Burgundies measured an average pH of 3.52.

A clear pattern begins to emerge. The pH of early Oregon Pinot Noirs was far too high. It is not surprising that most fell apart and failed to fulfill their promise. With a few notable exceptions, great Oregon Pinot Noir was more of a potential than an actuality.

This is not to say that low pH guarantees a great wine. Enough acidity can be added to any wine to achieve a low pH. Although low pH does not guarantee a wine will be great, high pH does guarantee that a wine will never be great.

How does a winegrower achieve lower pH? Most importantly, it starts in the vineyard. Not coincidentally, factors that play a role in achieving low pH are also associated with flavor intensity and complexity.

Overcropped vines are prone to higher pH as well as loss of fruit intensity. For Oregon Pinot Noir, a yield not exceeding three tons an acre is the rule-of-thumb for quality wine. Lower yields are even better, but financial concerns rapidly become an overriding issue.

Vine density is a factor, though how much is still not clear. Burgundian vineyards have 4,000 or more vines per acre. Oregon vineyards are usually far more densely planted than the American norm, but even the most densely planted Oregon vineyards rarely approach 2,000 vines per acre.

Older vines more consistently yield lower pH, better balanced, more flavorful grapes in difficult years.

Canopy management is a definite factor. Vine pruning, training, and trellising methods are being revised to allow more sunlight to strike the grapes and foliage. Eliminating excess vegetative growth is also a positive factor.

Picking early in warm vintages is critical. Grapes must be harvested before they get overripe and develop undesirable pruney flavors and excessively high pH. More than any other vineyard practice, this has the most immediate and direct effect on the quality, character, and pH of the grapes.

In the winery, the winemaker must monitor the acidity and pH carefully, ready to add acid as necessary to bring acidity and pH into line.

Although most Oregon winegrowers are now attuned to the appropriate winegrowing methods, not all are, and some are more attuned than others. So what do we look for when buying Pinot Noir for our cellar?

Avoid buying young Pinot Noir with an excessively soft, velvety texture. While such wines may be appealing to some tastes, they are not wines to cellar. The soft, smooth, "sweet" character indicates the wine has too little acid and too high of a pH. Tannin sometimes masks the softness, but it is not a cure for a poor acidity and pH.

Look for Pinot Noir with a good acid backbone. Although the wines should not taste nearly as hard and tannic as a young Cabernet Sauvignon, a certain youthful hardness is acceptable. Complexity and texture develop with age. A young Pinot Noir should not seem too soft and generous.

Wines from warm vintages usually are higher in alcohol. Because alcohol tends to make wine taste more rounded and less acidic, wines from warm vintages usually taste less hard. This is fine, the only caveat being that warm vintages are the ones most prone to overripeness, low acidity, and high pH.

A plummy character is typical of a warm vintage. The character is appropriate as long as it tends toward the black cherry/plummy end of the spectrum. If the plumminess begins to take on a pruney character, avoid the wine.

Pinot Noir is inherently less colored than other red grape varieties. A deep color is not a critical factor, but the color should be true. A young Pinot Noir should be a clarion purple-red, with no brownish or brickish coloration.

Young Pinot Noir should have good fruit intensity. Complexity and length may begin to show early, but sometimes the flavors can seem simple and direct at first.

Great Pinot Noir is made in the vineyard and winery, but it does not fulfill its greatness without time in the cellar. Old Burgundies can be remarkable wines, with an incredible array of flavors, textures, and scents.

The only examples of older Oregon Pinot Noir we have were made during an earlier era, when grape growing and winemaking practices were far less than ideal, and in some cases, just the opposite of what was needed. But a few Oregon Pinot Noirs from the early years, partially by intent of the pioneer visionaries, and partially because of happy accident, were made in a manner more closely approximating the practices of today. These wines have aged well and developed fine flavor and bouquet. They show clearly that truly fine Oregon Pinot Noir is more than just potential.

The good news is that the Oregon Pinot Noirs of today routinely and readily surpass the best wines of the earlier years. Oregon winegrowers are continuing to make rapid strides in grape and wine quality. But already, the wines of today are evidence that great Oregon Pinot Noir is more than just some far distant potential. Genuine greatness is at hand.

Thank you Oregon winegrowers for all you have done for us lovers of the world's most sublime grape. Our thanks, most especially, to the visionary winegrowing pioneers, and to those who later joined the journey along the path to greatness.

Bordeaux Nouveau— the Decline of a Standard

The following is an opinion. The opinion is by no means solitary, others share it, but it has been given relatively little voice in print. As a lover of fine wine, and particularly, fine Bordeaux, I do not voice this opinion with glee, but with a measure of sadness.

Classic Bordeaux, by historical precedent and inherent quality, has been the world standard for Cabernet Sauvignon (and the other Bordeaux grape varieties, most prominently, Merlot). For America and the rest of the New World, the great Bordeaux wines have, and still do, set the standard for the wine world. But, Bordeaux is becoming less and less an adequate model, less and less the standard for the world. New World Cabernet Sauvignon is rising in quality just as Bordeaux is declining. The new Bordeaux is becoming a muted echo of its former greatness.

Classic Bordeaux is hard in youth, fairly high in acid and tannins, with a rather angular structure to support a long life of development in the bottle. The unyielding nature of young classic Bordeaux makes possible the magnificent complex bouquets and flavors that come from aging in the bottle. Great Bordeaux is made by those who make wines for those who will wait.

But, more and more, Bordeaux is made for those who will not wait, those for whom two or three years in the cellar is too long, and five or ten years or more is out of the question. The new Bordeaux is a much softer wine, readily accessible in youth, fruity, low acid, tasty, and simple. It is a good drink, but not a great one. At its price, it is an insult.

The accountants and bean counters and owners want wines that can be released and consumed sooner, and turned into profits more quickly. They want consistency with no bad vintages, even if the new style means no truly great vintages either. Leveling all factors, including quality, down to a predictable, consistent norm is the commercial ideal.

Those who make the new Bordeaux tell us that these are still great wines, and maybe even better since we can enjoy them sooner. Since our modern day lifestyle is more hectic and transient, this is just what we would like to hear. It would be so convenient on all sides if these falsehoods were true.

Classic Bordeaux had very great vintages and very poor vintages. The new Bordeaux, with modern viticultural techniques and with winemaking practices heavily influenced by the highly acclaimed French enologist, Emile Peynaud, offers no bad vintages—but no really great vintages either.

The highly celebrated 1982 Bordeaux vintage demonstrates the new Bordeaux at its best—and thus, in a convoluted way, at its worst, demonstrating the inherent weaknesses of the new style. Classic Bordeaux is still made in Bordeaux, and to that extent, 1982 may still be a great vintage. For many chateau, however, 1982 meant wines with very rich, ripe flavors, low acid, a simple direct character, and little hope of the greatness that comes with cellaring classic Bordeaux.

The 1982 Bordeaux vintage was said to be rather California in character. To some extent this may be true, but it really does a disservice to the best of the current California Cabernet Sauvignon style. The excesses of the 1970s in California Cabernet have given way to an understanding that excessive ripeness does not lend itself to great wine, nor does high alcohol and low acid.

The best Northwest Cabernet Sauvignon (principally grown in Washington state's Columbia Valley), the best of California Cabernet, and classic Bordeaux have more in common amongst themselves than any of them have with the new Bordeaux.

Burgundy is routinely criticized for uneven and declining quality, yet Burgundy has been turning things around. Prices remain terribly high, but quality is improving. France is producing more and more truly fine Burgundy.

Bordeaux has long enjoyed the reputation of consistently exceptional quality. It is no longer deserved. Higher yields, less qualitatively desirable grape clones, overripeness, more routine chaptalization (yes, chaptalization in Bordeaux), and changing winemaking methods all conspire to diminish the quality of the new Bordeaux.

Since this is principally a book on the wines of America's Northwest, a slightly chauvinistic digression is in order. Cabernet Sauvignon from Washington's Columbia Valley, at its finest, is truly one of the brightest spots in New World Cabernet Sauvignon. The best possess an extraordinary intensity of color and varietal fruit, the absence of vegetative character, and a textural richness that meshes with good acids and a sturdy backbone.

Like classic Bordeaux, the best Washington Cabernet Sauvignons are fairly high in acid and tannin, yet they have a riper, fuller character not unlike the best of California Cabernet. Like classic Bordeaux, they absolutely need time in the cellar for their complexities to unfold. The better wines from even the lighter vintages may need a half dozen years or so to begin really showing their stuff.

This is not to say that all Washington Cabernet Sauvignons meet the highest standards of excellence. Lesser Washington Cabernets can be overripe and pruney, or display excessively berrylike, herbaceous, or burnt flavors. Yet, with with only a couple dedicated decades of winemaking, the best Washington Cabernet Sauvignon is already in the qualitative forefront of New World Cabernet Sauvignon. The advances in just the past few years promise even greater heights.

Some Bordeaux are still made in the classic style, still set the standards of greatness. Thank you. Most are too expensive for me to buy, but thank you anyway. It is good to know that quality has not been completely forsaken for expediency.

And thank you New World. You deserve a better standard, a better target, than the new Bordeaux, but the best Cabernet Sauvignon from California, Washington, and southern Oregon are doing fine honor to a classic tradition.

Fresh & Fruity versus Rich & Complex

Wine styles can be divided into two broad categories, fresh and fruity, and rich and complex. Red wines are usually made in a rich and complex style, like the typical Cabernet Sauvignon, Pinot Noir, Bordeaux, and Burgundy wines. Beaujolais Nouveau is an example of one of the relatively few red wines made in the fresh and fruity style. White wines vary more widely, some made in the extreme fresh and fruity style, like the typical Washington Riesling. Others are made in a rich and complex style, like French White Burgundies, many Oregon Chardonnays, and a few Washington Chardonnays.

The style of a wine is determined by the grape variety and growing conditions, and by the choice of winemaking methods. We will look at the characteristics of different grape varieties later on, but first let's examine winemaking choices that determine where on the stylistic spectrum a wine will fall, from radically fresh and fruity, to radically rich and complex, to somewhere in between. Since white wines are more subject to these stylistic decisions, our discussion will focus on them, but the same principals apply to red wines as well.

Having the best of both worlds would be wonderful, but the fresher and more like the fruit of the grape a wine tastes, the more one dimensional and less enduring on the palate and in the cellar it becomes. Conversely, the more rich and complex a wine is, the less it tastes like the lively engaging fruit of the grape. Winemakers can, and often do, choose both fresh and fruity and rich and complex methods to make a wine that falls somewhere between the radical ends of the spectrum.

The table of winemaking methods in this chapter is by no means a complete exposition of winemaking choices, but it illustrates some of the basic methods that determine whether a wine will have fresher, fruitier characteristics, or will tend toward the richer, fuller, more complex end of the spectrum.

Grape varieties themselves have intrinsic characteristics that respond best to certain winemaking choices. Riesling and Chardonnay are traditionally considered the world's two greatest white wine grapes. Coincidentally, the two grapes represent the opposite ends of the character spectrum.

Riesling is inherently floral and fruity with a highly defined varietal profile. Its claim to greatness relies, at least in part, on its fruity qualities. Riesling grapes taste much like Riesling wine. To bring out the best in Riesling, most winemakers choose "fresh and fruity" winemaking methods.

Chardonnay is quite the opposite. Unlike Riesling, Chardonnay is not highly fruity, nor does it have a high varietal profile. Its claim to greatness is its subtle, manifold, flavor complexities and textures.

Making Riesling wines is largely a process of non-interference with the fruit of the grape. Absolute emphasis on fresh and fruity winemaking methods might be modified slightly if the wine is meant for long aging, as with certain German or Alsatian Rieslings, but winemaking methods for Riesl-

Fresh & Fruity versus Rich & Complex

Fresh & Fruity
• Fermentation in stainless steel.
• Low fermentation temperatures.
• Absence of oxygen during fermentation and aging.
• Quick removal of lees and other solids.
• No malolactic fermentation.
• Little or no aging in oak barrels.
• A neutral yeast, or one that emphasizes fruitiness.
• Dissolved carbon dioxide in the finished wine.

Rich & Complex
• Fermentation in oak barrels.
• High fermentation temperatures.
• Controlled oxygenation during fermentation and aging.
• Lengthy lees contact.
• Malolactic fermentation.
• Lengthy barrel aging.
• A less neutral yeast, producing rounder, fuller wines.
• No spritzy carbon dioxide in the finished wine.

ing are typically chosen entirely from the "fresh and fruity" column.

Chardonnay is a winemaker's grape. Rather than a process of non-interference, the task of the Chardonnay winemaker is to work with the complex, textural subtleties of the grape. Classic Chardonnays, typified by the great French White Burgundies, are made by building on and fleshing out the basic framework of the grape. Chardonnay is not particularly fruity, so little is lost in this approach, and much is gained. Classic Chardonnays draw heavily from the "rich and complex" column of winemaking methods.

Oregon winemakers, within the context of their winegrowing climate, produce Chardonnays in the classic style. Curiously, most Washington winemakers draw more heavily from the "fresh and fruity" column of winemaking methods. A typical Washington Chardonnay might be fermented at an intermediate temperature in stainless steel tanks, racked quickly off the lees, prevented from going through a malolactic fermentation, then aged a short time in oak.

As nice as the typical Washington Chardonnay is, it does not really show the grape at its best. Fruity Washington Chardonnay is most certainly a valid style. It effectively demonstrates the intense fruitiness of the region's wines, and expands the range of wines and wine styles available to us, but it is not the ultimate rendition of the grape. Happily, more and more Washington winemakers are moving more toward the rich and complex end of the stylistic spectrum, and showing the grape and the region at their best.

At the same time, we should not argue for a monotheistic approach to winemaking. I have taken pleasure in unusual Chardonnays made in the style of a German Riesling and unusual Rieslings made in the style of a French White Burgundy. While such wines may not bring out the ultimate in the grape, they can be pleasurable and different, and thus enrich our world of wine.

We have discussed how wine can be categorized into two broad styles, how winemaking methods bring about these styles, and how the intrinsic characteristics of grape varieties can be enhanced by winemaking choices that complement their nature. These categories and methods help us understand the flavors in wine and winemaking choices, but they should not be regarded as a regimented formula. The art of winemaking is a subtle weaving of methods, a complex dialog with the fruit of the vintage.

Northwest Vintages

Everything that grows has "vintages," from apples to alfalfa, grain to grapes. The character of fine teas differ discernibly from vintage to vintage. The more esthetically complex the product of the land, the more pronounced are the differences from vintage to vintage.

Perhaps no product of the land and climate is more esthetically rich than wine grapes and wine. It is no wonder then, that for wine, above all, we speak of vintages and vintage years.

But it is also no wonder, given our preoccupation with quantification and quasi-objectification, even in matters of esthetics, that we try to reduce the complex weaving of flavors and scents and characteristics, that are the products of land and climate and vintage, to a numeric scale. These simplistic reductions inevitably conceal as much as they reveal.

In a general sense, we can sometimes legitimately say that one vintage is better than another, or that one vintage is particularly outstanding or notably less good. But often, vintages are not simply better or less good than one another. Vintages differ in complex ways that are not always reducible to conceptions of better and best. Each vintage is a collection of characteristics and tendencies. Unless extreme, the collection of characteristics will seldom insure that a vintage will be poor or great.

In a warm vintage, for example, an excellent red wine will tend to be rich and concentrated with lots of extract. A less successful wine might tend to be overripe, pruney, and flat tasting, without good acidity or structure. Even though qualitatively quite different, both wines would reflect the character of the vintage. In a cool vintage, an excellent wine will tend to have a perfumed fruity elegance with a good acid structure for aging. A less successful wine might tend to be thin, overly acidic, with little fruit or character.

In any vintage, the winegrower's task is to bring the best out of the tendencies of the vintage, to emphasize the strengths and minimize the weaknesses.

Descriptions of vintages can only be broad generalizations. Without fail, wines in every vintage defy the general character or quality level of the vintage. There are enough differences in microclimates, viticultural practices, and winemaking skills and methods to insure that, inevitably, excellent wines are made in poor vintages and poor wines are made in excellent vintages.

Understanding vintage differences helps us understand and appreciate fine wine, but if we simply look at a vintage chart and buy or reject wine according to numeric ratings, we do ourselves and the cause of fine wines an injustice. The old adage speaks clearly and succinctly—*BUY WINES NOT VINTAGES.*

With these caveats in mind, here are some vintage comments. Red wines, as a general rule, more directly reflect the character of the vintage than white wines, and red wines are usually cellared longer than whites. For these reasons, the commentary is more heavily weighted toward red wines. Except as noted, the comments are focused on western Oregon, primarily the Willamette Valley, and the Columbia Valley in Washington, the major grape growing areas in the two states.

Oregon

1977

A cool and ungenerous vintage. The wines tended to be thin and hard. A very few of the Pinot Noirs had good fruit. Because of their naturally high acidity, they aged well, and demonstrated the importance of acidity and structure for better winemaking approaches that would come in later years.

1978

A hot year. Coming after a difficult cool year, and at a time in the history of the industry when most Oregon winegrowers were still seeking maximum sugars, the grapes were allowed to overripen. A few good Chardonnays in a big style were made. The Pinot Noirs, with only rare exception, were overripe, pruney, high alcohol, and low acid.

pH readings of more than 4.0 were not uncommon in Pinot Noir. Any initial charm the wines may have had faded as quickly as they browned. The grapes were picked too late and not enough saving acid was added in the winemaking process. The year was a benchmark of how not to make wine in a hot Oregon vintage.

1979

The year was very warm, but not as extreme as '78. Crop levels were high, many new wineries came into production, and it was an easy year to make good wine. Although much more successful overall than '78, the wines, nevertheless, suffered many of the same failings, though in a more subtle, less intrusive way.

Many of the Pinot Noirs were high pH and did not age well, though they had a certain full, generous, and fruity character when young. The vintage had been highly regarded, but in retrospect, the enthusiasm was not entirely warranted.

1980

A cool wet spring, followed by a cool growing season, yielded grapes with generally low sugar levels. As always, there are exceptions, but throughout western Oregon, the wines were generally light and unfocused.

1981

Cool wet weather in spring and early summer caused a late start on the season and a poor crop set. The rest of summer and early fall was warm. Some areas were hit by an extreme heat wave in August. The rains returned as harvest approached, and some vineyards suffered severe bunch rot, further reducing the crop.

Sugar levels were variable, but generally fairly low. The grapes had a certain concentration because of the small crop but still lacked a fullness of flavors. Many excellent Rieslings came out of the vintage, but, overall, it was a mediocre year for most wines.

1982

Following two difficult vintages and the low yields of the '81 vintage, 1982 was a welcome one for grape growers. Good grape prices and a very heavy crop meant money in the bank. The unexpectedly heavy crop, however, had its downside. Overcropped vines meant grapes and wines that sometimes lacked intensity. The wines were routinely good, if not great, but winegrowers who pruned to reduce yields were able to produce excellent wines.

1983

A highly acclaimed Pinot Noir vintage. Many winemakers regarded 1983 as their finest Pinot Noir vintage ever. Successful and highly publicized comparative tastings with French Burgundies further fueled the regard for the vintage. Moderate yields, small berries, and a warm, sunny, fall, ripening period translated into concentrated wines.

The initial excitement over the vintage was, for the most part, justified. But, in retrospect, a few of the Pinot Noirs showed some evidence of a plummy quality edging into a pruney character, indicating slight overripeness. The pHs are somewhat high for wines that are expected to age into greatness. Overall, however, it was an excellent vintage for Pinot Noir as well as the other varieties.

1984

A cold, rainy vintage made a miserable year for grape grower and winemaker alike. Low sugars, high acids, and unripe fruit meant thin wines with little character. A lot of the Pinot Noir was turned into Pinot Noir Blanc—a palatable off-dry white wine. It was a good year to test the skills of the winegrower, a year that showed who could make good wines under difficult conditions.

There were, however, a few fine wines made in '84, some good Chardonnays, and at least a couple of excellent Pinot Noirs that promise to cellar well and surpass many of the highly regarded '83 Pinot Noirs. Although the majority of '84s were below average quality, the successes emphasize the importance of the adage, "buy wines, not vintages."

1985

A spring frost hit southwest Oregon, and, unusually, many of the less than ideal sites in the Willamette Valley, reducing crop yields. A dry, warm, growing season meant smaller berries, less vine growth, and concentrated, well-balanced wine grapes.

There was some concern that the warm vintage would be like the unfortunate '78 vintage, but grape acids held, and the more astute winemakers picked before the grapes became overripe. The net result was an exceptional vintage, particularly for Pinot Noir, which had lower pHs than the highly regarded '83 vintage and generally surpassed it in quality. The best '85 Pinot Noirs are sometimes less perfumed than the Pinots of more typical vintages, but they are rich, concentrated, and deeply colored, with excellent structure for aging.

1986

What looked like a warm early harvest was thwarted by September rains. Winegrowers who picked before or during the rains and chaptalized, generally made less good wines than those who waited out the rain. Early grape varieties and young vineyards were more affected by the rain. Quality is variable, but the best of the vintage are excellent wines, well-balanced, with fine style and length.

1987

One of the warmest vintages and earliest harvests on record. Winemakers who wisely picked according to acid and pH, rather than sugar, sometimes received grapes that were low in sugar and not very darkly colored. Those, who did not monitor their vineyards closely, picked overripe grapes, but most growers fared much better.

A decade ago, a vintage like this would have produced grossly overripe, high alcohol, high pH, low acid, pruney Pinot Noirs. Now, however, Oregon winemakers are much more knowledgeable at handling very cool and very warm vintages, and 1987 promises another year of good quality, if not typical, wines.

Washington

1977

A cooler vintage that yielded red wines with a tight edged structure. The few red wines made during the vintage have aged well.

1978

A warm vintage with sometimes badly overcropped vines. A few of the wines were a bit too ripe, but those that were cropped more conservatively, and picked timely, showed fine concentration and flavors.

1979

Following one of the most severe winters on record, the grape crop was greatly reduced. The summer was very warm, and harvest came early.

The best Cabernet Sauvignons are excellent wines, intense, concentrated, and long-lived. Others have a raisined, cooked character, and will forever be unbalanced. Some are intense and hard, but lack fruit or charm. The color was so intense in some red wines, they were virtually black. The white wines generally suffered from excess heat.

1980

A cool growing season, sugar levels were generally lower and acids higher than average. Although the vintage generally lacks the concentrated intensity that is the hallmark of the finest vintages, it yielded many well-balanced wines. Though ready to drink earlier than most vintages, the red wines have aged very well, developing good bottle-aged character and showing a fine textural suppleness.

1981

The second consecutive growing season with below average temperatures. A cool wet spring delayed the start of the season, but warm temperatures in late summer and early fall brought the grapes in balance. Cooling temperatures, as harvest began, extended the growing season.

Overall, the wines were flavorful and well balanced, with a better focus than the 1980 vintage. The red wines have a harder edge than those from warmer years, but an excellent structure for long aging, and should continue to develop well.

1982

Good summer weather was followed by unusual fall rains and some problems with rot. Overall, 1982 was a good Washington vintage. The red wines were rounder and more supple than those of 1981, but some were higher in pH than desirable.

1983

An early fall frost defoliated some vineyards, cutting short complete ripening of the grapes, but, overall, the vintage showed fine fruit with good, crisp, acid levels. It was an excellent vintage for red wines. They showed concentrated fruit character, and good acid and tannin structure, without sacrificing texture and suppleness.

1984

The previous year's fall frost, winter damage to the vines, a cool spring, and less good berry set contributed to a reduced grape crop. The season's late start delayed harvest. Final ripening of the grapes took place in cooler than normal conditions. Sugars were somewhat lower and acids higher, but the reduced crop and smaller berries meant good fruit character in many vineyards.

As if to prove that vintage generalizations are merely that, one winery sold off a batch of Cabernet Sauvignon wine it made from overripe grapes, and another winery produced its first port from what would be, from a dry table wine perspective, greatly overripe grapes with excessively high sugars.

Some winemakers complained of underripe grapes, while others found the fruit excellent. Some of the red wines were light and lacked concentration. Others showed excellent fruit character and an elegance reminiscent of traditionally made Bordeaux, with promise of excellent aging potential.

1985

A series of spring frosts damaged the vines and reduced the grape crop. Because some of the grapes came from the secondary buds, after the primary buds had been damaged, grape ripeness on damaged vines was often uneven. The summer was hot, and the harvest started very early, in late August. Early September rains and cool weather extended the harvest before a series of fall frosts closed out the growing season.

A small crop and small berries usually mean concentrated varietal fruit, but the hot growing season and early harvest was an opposite influence. Wine quality is variable, depending on individual circumstances. The quality ranges from big, clumsy, below average wines, lacking fruit complexity, to well-structured, richly concentrated wines of above average quality.

1986

An unusual vintage, very cool months were followed by very hot months. Overall, it was one of the state's warmer vintages. As the early harvest was beginning in September, atypical heavy rains hit, delaying harvest. The cloudy rainy weather disrupted the Columbia Valley's classic final ripening cycle, of warm sunny days followed by cold nights, which is critical to good sugars, fruit character, and crisp acids.

Many of the red wines will not have the focus and intensity of better years. The early fall rains, followed by an extended harvest and warm dry weather, however, made 1986 one of the finest vintages for botrytised Rieslings.

1987

The warmest vintage and one of the earliest harvests in two decades. Harvest began in August for some grape varieties. In spite of the hot, early season, the grapes generally showed good fruit character. Smaller than average berries contributed to the intensity and extract.

Wineries that picked early to avoid low acid, high pH wines sometimes found grapes that were not very darkly colored, with low to moderate sugars. Tartaric acid was in high demand to balance the sometimes very low acids. Fruit quality was surprisingly excellent for such a hot vintage. Not a classic Washington vintage, but a good one nonetheless.

Northwest Grapes

Unless otherwise noted, references to Oregon, Washington, or Idaho pertain to the major grape growing areas of each state, i.e., Oregon's Willamette and Umpqua Valleys, Washington's Columbia and Yakima Valleys, and Idaho's Snake River Valley.

Aligote

Grown in miniscule quantities in Washington, Aligote is a high yielding, lesser quality white grape of France's Burgundy region. It is generally similar to Chardonnay, though with a leaner profile and much less finesse. In Washington, it is sometimes blended with other wine with a stronger varietal character.

Auxerrois

A widely planted but little known Alsatian white grape variety may find a home in Oregon. Now only in experimental development, Auxerrois could fill a role as a good quality, everyday table wine.

Baco Noir

A red French-American hybrid grape planted in Washington's Columbia Valley at a time when there were doubts that premium vinifera wine grapes could survive the winters. Premium vinifera grapes now reign supreme. The French-American hybrid grapes, and the wineries that focused on them, have slipped into oblivion.

Cabernet Franc

Grown in miniscule quantities in Washington and Oregon, Cabernet Franc, one of the Bordeaux grape varieties, produces a wine very similar to Cabernet Sauvignon, though less intense, with typically lower acids and tannins. In such tiny quantities, it is almost always blended.

Cabernet Sauvignon

Arguably, Washington's finest wine grape. Washington Cabernets are typically deeply colored and flavored, full bodied, rough, and tannic when young, frequently needing several years of bottle age to begin showing their best.

Their sturdy structure and backbone is similar to classically styled Bordeaux, but with a ripeness and body more reminiscent of a California Cabernet. Ultimately, they are Cabernet Sauvignon in their own style.

The better Washington Cabernets avoid burnt and overtly weedy flavors. Sometimes, Washington Cabernet Sauvignons have a berry-like character that is atypical of Bordeaux or California Cabernet. The finest combine rich fruit with spicy flavors and scents. Supple, yet possessing a sturdy acid backbone, they are long-lived wines that require bottle aging to fully develop their potential.

Growing site is critical for the finest Washington Cabernet Sauvignon. Warmer sloped sites are best. Sub-regions and vineyards produce Cabernet Sauvignon with distinctive characteristics. The cooler areas tend to produce more of the berry-like or herbal flavors. Warmer areas are more textural and spicy.

With occasional exception, Oregon's Willamette Valley is too cool for the best Cabernet Sauvignon. Further south, the Umpqua Valley, and, particularly, southwest Oregon, near the California border, are capable of producing fine Cabernets.

Campbell Early

A native American, non-vinifera, red grape variety. *See Island Belle.*

Cascade

A red, French-American, hybrid grape planted in Washington's Columbia Valley at a time when there were doubts that premium vinifera wine grapes could survive the winters. Now that the much higher quality vinifera wine grapes have proven themselves, Cascade has slipped into oblivion.

Chardonnay

Oregon's premier white wine grape is also its most challenging. The predominant Chardonnay clone grown in the state was developed for warmer climates, but the Oregon winegrowers have effectively worked around its shortcomings.

Chardonnay is a winemaker's grape. Much of the final character of the wine depends on the winemaker's hand. In Oregon, traditional Burgundian winemaking methods predominate—relatively warm fermentation temperatures, barrel fermentation, lees contact, and the like. The best are elegant and complex wines, often delicate, yet rich in flavor with a sturdy acid backbone. It is a challenging grape, and some winemakers achieve the ideal more routinely than others.

Washington Chardonnays are routinely and reliably good, though often a bit simple and coarse compared to the best attainable from the grape. The choice of winemaking style seems more the culprit than any climatic constraint. Washington's predominant style treats the grape as if it were highly fruity and aromatic—which it is not. Cold fermentation temperatures, stainless steel tanks, avoidance of lees contact, and so on, are fine for Riesling, but not Chardonnay—at least not great Chardonnay.

There is a thankful trend to incorporate more of the traditional Burgundian winemaking methods into Washington Chardonnay. The efforts in this direction suggest that great Chardonnay from Washington is a genuine possibility.

Idaho Chardonnays are generally similar to those of Washington. The Chardonnay grape adapts well to a wide range of climates from very cool to quite warm. It has adapted well to Idaho's intense but relatively short growing season.

Chenin Blanc

In America, specifically, California, Chenin Blanc is considered a lowly varietal with little character. Though not a great grape, it is regarded far more highly in Europe.

Washington Chenin Blanc is usually made in a tasty, fresh, fruity style with some residual sweetness. Chenin Blanc also lends itself to a drier, wood-aged style. A few Washington Chenin Blancs are made in this style with good success.

Washington Chenin Blancs have considerably more interest than the typical examples from California, but the variety inherently yields high quantities of grapes, and most Washington grape growers do not discourage this tendency. Many Washington Chenin Blancs lack the focus and intensity that smaller yields would bring. Washington is capable of producing even better Chenin Blanc, but for now, the grape is stuck in its role as a high yielding variety for moderately priced, easy quaffing wines.

In Oregon and Southwest Washington, very little Chenin Blanc is produced, but some fine examples in a variety of styles add interest to the wine spectrum. Idaho also produces good Chenin Blanc, but the grape's lack of winter hardiness is even more of a problem than it is in Washington.

Concord

A native American variety with no merit as a wine grape. It is heavily planted in Washington's Yakima Valley for grape juice, jellies, and other such products.

Ehrenfelser

A German cross of Riesling and Sylvaner, planted in miniscule quantities in Oregon. It has a Riesling-like character but ripens earlier with less acidity.

Gamay Beaujolais

Once thought to be the grape of France's Beaujolais district, the Gamay Beaujolais grown in the Northwest and the rest of America is actually a clone of Pinot Noir and not a separate grape variety. *See Gamay Noir a Jus Blanc.*

Gamay Noir a Jus Blanc

The true Gamay grape of France's Beaujolais region, and a different grape than the Gamay and Gamay Beaujolais grown in America. Showing excellent promise in Oregon, the grape is beginning to find its way out of the experimental stage, into commercial plantings.

Like French Beaujolais, it promises high yields of fine quality, fruity, flavorful, red wine. The classic grape of nouveau wines, the true Gamay is also capable of more substantive wines of distinction.

Gewurztraminer

A fickle grape that needs the right climate and growing site to develop its spicy flavor intensity without turning flat and dull. It was one of Washington's earliest successful vinifera grape varieties.

Both Washington and Oregon produce good Gewurztraminer in styles from bone dry to slightly sweet. Washington also produces heavily botrytised sweet versions. The few examples from Idaho have shown good balance and fine, spicy, Gewurztraminer character. Some of the best Gewurztraminer grapes in the Northwest are grown along the Columbia Gorge, on either side of the Oregon-Washington border.

Grenache

The grape requires a very warm growing climate and a long season. Both along the Columbia Gorge and in Washington's Columbia Valley, Grenache produces good, soft, red wines and flavorful roses with pleasant flavors of black pepper and spice. There is little acreage in Washington, and expansion seems unlikely because of the grape's acute sensitivity to winter damage.

Island Belle

A local variant of the native American, non-vinifera, red grape, Campbell Early. Developed in the late 1800s by Adam Eckert, Island Belle enjoyed commercial success as a table, jelly, and wine grape. Grown in western Washington's Puget Sound area, Island Belle fell out of favor when Columbia Valley Concord began to dominate the grape market. Except for those who find favor with its distinctive non-vinifera character, it is not a very good wine grape.

Lemberger

Another spelling of Limberger. *See Limberger.*

Limberger

Also spelled Lemberger, the variety is a little-known red wine grape grown in small quantities in several European countries. Limberger has become a speciality grape of Washington. The wines are darkly colored, with flavors of berries and vanilla. The character is straightforward without the texture or complexity of the great wine grapes, but the wines are, nevertheless, fruity, well-balanced, and tasty.

The variety can be cropped higher than other red varieties while still retaining balance and character. Limberger is a good grape for moderately priced red wines. Acreage is gradually expanding.

Madeleine Angevine

Also spelled Madeline Angevine, this cool climate grape is grown in western Washington's Puget Sound region. It is a French, vinifera, white grape bred in the Loire Valley in the 1850s from two older vinifera varieties, Precoce de Malingre and Madeleine Royale.

The wines range in style from dry to slightly sweet. Occasionally, sweet botrytised versions are made. The wines have good fruit character. The flavors are vaguely reminiscent of Semillon, with an added spicy component. Some of the current examples suggest excellent promise for the grape in Washington's Puget Sound area.

Marechal Foch

A French-American hybrid once planted in Washington before premium vinifera grapes buried all interest in hybrid varieties. It is currently released commercially in Oregon in very small quantities, and yields a dark colored red wine with unexpectedly (given its hybrid origins) fine flavors.

The grape is widely planted in the eastern United States, where it has a less than stellar reputation. A key to its success in Oregon seems to be the higher level of ripeness it achieves. In the warmer Oregon vintages, it has little of the hybrid taste.

Merlot

One of the Bordeaux grape varieties, Merlot marries well with Cabernet Sauvignon, contributing texture and suppleness. It is a highly regarded grape, but on its own, whether in Bordeaux, California, or the Northwest, it often comes across as if it were Cabernet Sauvignon lacking in varietal intensity.

Washington produces fine Merlot with good character and structure. Washington Cabernet Sauvignons from some growing sites can be very hard. Blending in Merlot gives them a more complete, less austere profile. Merlot ripens earlier than Cabernet Sauvignon, and can quickly become overripe if care is not taken at harvest time. After Cabernet Sauvignon, Merlot is Washington's finest red wine grape.

Very little Merlot is grown in Oregon. Unless the spring weather is just right, Merlot refuses to set berries. In Oregon, during berry set, conditions are seldom just right. Southwest Oregon, near the California border, experiences these problems to a lesser degree.

Morio Muskat

Also spelled Morio Muscat, the grape is grown in miniscule quantities in Washington. A cross between Sylvaner and Pinot Blanc, Morio Muskat ripens early and produces high yields. The appealing wines have an intense muscat flavor and aroma.

Muller-Thurgau

This century-old German crossing of Riesling and Sylvaner is, today, Germany's most widely planted grape. In Germany, Muller-Thurgau is typically cropped high and picked early to offer large quantities of inoffensive Liebfraumilch. Muller-Thurgau may not be the world's greatest white wine grape, but it is capable of better wines than the German norm.

If cropped conservatively and allowed to ripen in a very cool growing climate, Muller-Thurgau produces flavorful fruity wines with a pronounced floral-musky aroma. In most years, western Oregon is a bit too warm to bring out the best of the grape. Western Washington's Puget Sound area is a more ideal climate. The wines are best drunk young, while they are at their fruity and aromatic best.

Muscat Alexandria

One of the world's oldest grape varieties, Muscat Alexandria lacks refinement, even for a Muscat. The fruit lacks a clarion grapy voice, and the character is slightly earthy. Grown in Washington, the variety has been all but superseded by the superior Muscat Canelli.

Muscat Canelli

The principal Muscat grown in Washington. The grape has a variety of names, including Muscat Blanc and Muscat Frontignan. Its white wines have an intense aroma, and a luscious, fresh, fruity, muscat character. Washington's excellent Muscat Canellis are usually made in a sweet style. The vines are sensitive to cold damage, and are often one of the hardest hit varieties in a bad winter.

Muscat Ottonel

A white wine grape grown in tiny quantities in Oregon, Muscat Ottonel is of relatively recent origins. Bred in France's Loire region in the 1800s, Muscat Ottonel does well in cool climates, unlike other Muscat varieties. It is now the predominant Muscat of France's Alsace region. Its wines are less intensely muscat than other Muscats, and thus, to some tastes, less overt and more refined. Oregon's only commercial release of the grape is finished in a dry style, and offers a welcome addition to the wine spectrum.

Nebbiolo

The great red wine grape of Italy's Piedmont region is barely out of the experimental stage in Washington. If its potential is fully realized, Nebbiolo could become one of the state's finest wine grapes. Its success is not yet known, but early assessment is hopeful.

Okanogan Riesling

Also spelled Okanagan Riesling, this traditional Canadian white wine grape has made its way south to western Washington. Of uncertain origin, the grape is now generally believed to be an interspecific hybrid and not a true vinifera. Although Washington efforts have been very successful in taming its sometimes coarse nature, the grape is not likely to play a major role in the future of the western Washington wine industry.

Petite Sirah

Once thought to be the noble Syrah grape of France's Rhone region, Petite Sirah is now know to be the considerably less noble Durif grape. Making its way north from California, there have been commercial releases of Washington Petite Sirah, but the grape has not generated much interest. Petite Sirah wines are darkly colored, big, tannic, and rather dull, lacking in fruit. They have fine structure, but offer no special flavor or character.

Pinot Gris

A genetic relative of Pinot Noir. Virtually non-existent in the rest of America, Pinot Gris has become one of Oregon's speciality grape varieties. The grape is grown in a wide range of European countries, but its best known wines are from France's Alsace region, where it is also known as Tokay d'Alsace.

At its worst, Pinot Gris offers a heavy, flat, dull white wine. At its best, Pinot Gris is a crisp, full-bodied, full-flavored wine of distinction. Oregon's best renditions of the grape are finished dry, and strike a balance between the extremes of crisp and simple, and heavy and flat. Early picking in warm vintages helps maintain the wine's balance. Unlike some white wines that seem hollow without oak, Pinot Gris is complete even when it has seen only stainless steel.

Pinot Meunier

Grown in miniscule quantities in Oregon, the grape is a red relative of Pinot Noir. It plays a major role in French Champagne, but is of much less interest as a red wine grape.

Pinot Noir

Oregon Pinot Noir is arguably the Northwest's finest wine. Unlike the Cabernet Sauvignon grape, which produces fine wines throughout the world, Pinot Noir, the great red grape of Burgundy, rarely produces wines of distinction outside its French homeland. Pinot Noir is by far the most sensitive of the great wine grapes. If growing conditions are not just right, Pinot Noir becomes nondescript, at best, or develops less desirable, and sometimes unpleasant, flavors and scents.

Oregon's Willamette Valley meets the grape's criteria with perfection. Although the cooler growing regions of California produce good Pinot Noir, the wines rarely have the length, finesse, or complexity of Oregon's best. California's famed Carneros region is a cooler area of a very warm climate. Oregon more closely matches the Burgundian norm, growing Pinot Noir on the warmer sites of a cool growing region.

In California, Pinot Noir ripens in the heat of late summer. In Oregon, the grapes ripen in moderating fall temperatures. This extended period of ripening, under moderate conditions, develops and retains the complex flavors of great Pinot Noir.

In the earlier years of the Oregon wine industry, there were fears that the Willamette Valley was too cool for the best wine grapes. But, if anything, in some years the climate may be a bit too warm for Pinot Noir. High pH, low acid, overripe Pinot Noirs were a product of earlier Oregon wine-growing practices. Improved grape growing and winemaking methods have made these concerns less frequent, and warm vintages less troublesome.

The excellent Oregon Pinot Noirs of today are eloquent testimony to the greatness of Oregon Pinot Noir. The purchase, in 1987, of nearly 100 acres of vineyard land in the Willamette Valley by Robert Drouhin of France's respected Burgundian wine firm, Joseph Drouhin, is further evidence of the quality and significance of Oregon Pinot Noir.

Already, the finest Oregon Pinot Noirs are outstanding, but the best is still to come. Further advances in grape growing and winemaking practices are on the near horizon.

Like California, Washington's Columbia Valley occasionally produces good Pinot Noir, but the area is really not well suited to the grape. Idaho, too, looks doubtful. Southwest Washington, an extension of what is geologically known as the Willamette Trough, is effectively part of the Willamette Valley climate. This corner of Washington can authentically lay claim to quality Pinot Noir.

Riesling

Also known as White Riesling and Johannisberg Riesling, it is by far the most widely planted wine grape in the Northwest.

Riesling is a winegrower's dream. It is the most winter hardy of all the vinifera grape varieties, produces good yields, and grows successfully in a wide range of growing sites, from the coolest areas of Washington's Yakima and Oregon's Willamette Valleys, to Idaho's Snake River Valley, to the very warm Wahluke Slope in Washington's Columbia Valley. Riesling is a late season grape, but it develops varietal character early in the ripening cycle. Good Riesling can be made in a wide range of climates.

Washington and Idaho Rieslings tend toward a riper, fuller-bodied style, with more honeyed, muscat-like tendencies. Oregon Rieslings tend more toward the delicate and floral end of the spectrum. These differences are only general tendencies. It is quite possible to find delicate, floral, Washington Rieslings as well as ripe, honeyed, Oregon Rieslings.

The typical and ubiquitous Northwest Riesling is made in a crisp fruity style, with some residual sweetness. Some of the most interesting Northwest Riesling are made in a wide range of less common styles—bone dry, intensely sweet and botrytised, ice wines, sparkling, and even barrel fermented and barrel aged on the lees.

The finest Northwest Rieslings occasionally approximate the elusive balance of ripeness, refinement, crisp acidity, and complex flavors and scents that is the hallmark of the finer Rieslings from Germany or those from France's Alsace region. In America, except perhaps for the Rieslings of the Northeast, they have no equal. Most Northwest Rieslings, however, are simply good, if not particularly exciting wines. Today, particularly in Washington, Riesling is in oversupply relative to the other grape varieties.

Sauvignon Blanc

Also known as Fume Blanc, Sauvignon Blanc has evolved into a fashionable grape, both in America and in Europe. Grown throughout the Northwest, it is a major variety only in Washington. Sauvignon Blanc has an herbaceous, grassy, varietal character. It also has a character that British enophiles, affectionately and with a reasonable measure of accuracy, describe as cat's piss. It is a very good wine grape, yet its current fashion exceeds its quality.

Sauvignon Blanc plays a role in white Bordeaux, where it adds fragrance and freshness to Semillon, Bordeaux's true, great, white wine grape. Sauvignon Blanc has a direct, simple, rather coarse character. It rarely develops well with bottle aging, and is usually best when consumed young. Sauvignon Blanc stands up better to warm growing climates than the more subtle and complexly flavored Semillon. Partly because of this, it emerged in California, and thus, in America, as a supposedly superior grape to Semillon.

Current fashion, in the Northwest as well as California, calls for grape growing and winemaking methods that minimize its herbaceous characteristics.

What are purportedly dry Sauvignon Blancs are often finished with slight residual sweetness for a rounder, less cutting profile. Such wines can become quite cloying during the course of a meal, as they warm and the sweetness becomes more apparent.

Sauvignon Blanc is really at its best when made bone dry, with some wood aging to tame the herbaceous element and add complexity. It is perhaps at its best when blended in small quantities with Semillon. Sauvignon Blanc is genuinely a very good wine grape—just not a great wine grape as current fashion seems to suggest.

Semillon

In America, and more specifically, in California, Semillon is viewed as a lesser, secondary grape of white Bordeaux—as a grape of modest distinction that is not in the same league as Sauvignon Blanc. Quite the opposite is the case. Semillon is the predominate grape in great white Bordeaux. Sauvignon Blanc plays only a secondary role, adding a fresh aromatic element, or, in larger proportions, for providing aggressive flavors for lesser wines meant for early consumption.

Semillon is a far more subtle grape that develops increasing complexity with age in the cellar, but it can be flat and dull if it is grown in a climate that is too warm. Because the warmer California growing climates burn away much of Semillon's character, the more aggressive flavors of Sauvignon Blanc have been a necessary substitute for the superior Semillon. In fairness, some California growing climates also do well with Semillon.

Washington and southern Oregon produce excellent Semillon, but it is widely grown only in Washington. Washington Semillons are not shy in character. Some growing sites offer Semillon with a pronounced grassy character. The best Semillons offer the subtle complexity that is their hallmark in Bordeaux.

The potential of Washington Semillon is far from realized. One of the first commercial vinifera varieties, Semillon has only recently gained popularity. The wine is typically made in a fresh style with no wood aging. It is sometimes even subjected to being finished with some residual sweetness.

Semillon is benefited greatly by more traditional winemaking methods, particularly, wood aging, as well as warmer fermentation temperatures, lees contact, and the like. The Northwest already produces very fine Semillon. Great Semillon awaits a change in winemaking practices.

Siegerrebe

A German vinifera cross that makes very good white wine in western Washington's cool Puget Sound area. The grapes ripen with high sugars, low acids, and an intense spicy character. It is capable of producing very good, sweet botrytised wines.

Sylvaner

Grown only in very small quantities in Oregon, Sylvaner offers a slightly earthy, moderately flavored, Riesling-like wine.

Syrah

The great red grape of France's Rhone Valley is being grown only experimentally in Washington. If the grape proves suitable, it could become one of the Northwest's great wine grapes.

Zinfandel

Although the basis for many jug wines and the ubiquitous White Zinfandel, it can also be an exceptionally fine wine grape, as many examples from California have shown. Unfortunately, Zinfandel requires a long, warm, growing season, and is not well suited to Northwest climates.

In miniscule quantities, Zinfandel is grown in Washington's Columbia Valley, along the Columbia Gorge, and in southern Oregon. Occasionally, when the growing site and conditions are favorable, Zinfandel can produce very good wines in the Northwest. Unfortunately, those devoted to fine Zinfandel will most often have to look to California.

Companion Encyclopedia

Acetic Acid

The acid in vinegar. Also referred to in general terms as volatile acidity, or V.A. All wines have some acetic acid, and, to a limited extent, V.A. adds to a wine's complexity, but if V.A. is present to a discernible degree, the wine is flawed. *See acidity.*

Acidity

An important element in wine. Without adequate acidity, wine tastes flat and lifeless. A wine too high in acid will taste sharp and tart. Alcohol and sugar decrease the perception of acidity.

Wine also tastes less acid when consumed with food. A wine that seemed well balanced at a tasting where little food was consumed may later taste dull when served with the evening meal. Conversely, tasters, and even professional judges, may not always adequately account for the absence of food at a tasting, thereby rating excellent food wines lower than they might deserve.

The ultimate test of a dry wine is its ability to complement a fine meal, cleanse the palate, harmonize with the food, and remain interesting throughout the repast. In this, acidity plays a key role.

Acidity also plays a key role in a wine's ability to age and develop in the bottle. Tannin, alcohol, sugar, and acid all help wine age. Bordeaux, Port, Sauternes, and Moselle are examples of wines that emphasize one or more of these components, but none of the components, except acid, is absolutely necessary for the aging process.

The desired acid level in a wine is partially a matter of accustomed taste. European wines are generally higher in acid than California wines. Northwest wines are blessed with inherently higher acid levels similar to European wines.

These distinctions are sometimes muted by winemaking methods. Recent California Cabernet Sauvignons, for example, are often released with higher acidity (through acid addition, as necessary) similar to classic Bordeaux. Conversely, many recent Bordeaux wines are made in a new, softer style, with low acid levels. *See acetic acid, pH, malolactic fermentation, and total acidity.*

Ahtanum Ridge

The northwestern boundary of Washington's Yakima Valley. Most Yakima Valley vineyards are on moderate slopes on the eastern side of the Yakima River. The Ahtanum Ridge's more steeply sloped Red Willow Vineyard is among the best, and one of the most unique, in the Yakima Valley.

Allier Oak

A type of French oak. Because Allier oak has a tighter grain structure than Limousin oak, wines aged in Allier barrels take on oak flavors more slowly. Allier oak is often favored for wines that will have a long stay in barrels, require a firm component from the oak, but restrained and refined oak flavors. Allier oak is often favored by Oregon winemakers for their Pinot Noir.

American Oak

American white oak is a different species than the French oaks. Its character is inherently more aggressive, a feature that can either be exaggerated or reduced in the barrel manufacturing process. Some American oak barrels impart a taste only subtly distinguishable from other oaks. Others impart a very pronounced "whiskey-barrel" character, or strong vanilla-coconut flavors. New American oak barrels are much cheaper than French oak barrels, and are much easier on the budget in the difficult business of running a winery.

Because of the oak's strong character, it is seldom the choice for white wines, and is usually too intrusive for the more subtle red wines, such as Pinot Noir. It finds its tradition and home with American Cabernet Sauvignon. American oak is so associated with American Cabernet Sauvignon, that some wine drinkers regard the taste of Cabernet Sauvignon and American oak as one. They find lacking, wines that do not have the pronounced American oak character.

American oak marries well with the flavors of Cabernet Sauvignon and Merlot, but French oaks continue to gain increasing favor. Wineries, desiring the benefits of barrel aging without strong oak character, sometimes obtain used, neutralized, American oak whiskey barrels. This practice may sound less than noble, but excellent wines have come from such barrels.

American Winegrowers

The predecessor of Chateau Ste. Michelle. Immediately following Repeal of Prohibition, two wineries, Nawico and Pommerelle, began producing wine. In 1954, the two wineries merged to form American Winegrowers.

Seeing that the direction of the Washington wine industry was moving toward premium vinifera grape wines, American Winegrowers made a Semillon, Cabernet Sauvignon, Pinot Noir, and Grenache Rose in the 1967 vintage. The wines were released under a new label, Ste. Michelle.

Anthocyanins

The principal coloring pigments in red wines. *Vitis vinifera* grapes, the species responsible for the world's premium wine grapes, have up to eight or nine anthocyanins. Hybrids and other grape species have as many as 18 anthocyanins. The proportions of the pigments differ even among the grape varieties of the same species.

Pinot Noir is unusual in that some of the pigments are totally absent. True Pinot Noir is usually more lightly colored and differently shaded than other red grape varieties. Cabernet Sauvignon not only has a greater number of different anthocyanins than Pinot Noir, but quantitatively more as well—about twice as much. Wine drinkers often use color intensity as an indicator of wine quality in red wines. Applying this criteria across variety types diminishes the validity of the indicator. *See color.*

Applegate Valley

One of the warmest grape growing areas in western Oregon, the Applegate Valley, near the California border, has a shorter, more intense growing season than other parts of western Oregon. Unlike the Willamette Valley to the north, the threat of frosts is routine. Cabernet Sauvignon rather than Pinot Noir is the red wine grape of choice.

Aroma

The smell of the fruit of the grape. More pronounced in young wines, the aroma of a wine gives way to other smells and scents as the wine ages. Certain grape varieties, such as Riesling, have highly distinctive aromas.

More of the aroma of the grape is preserved by a winemaking style that emphasizes cool fermentations in stainless steel, no malolactic fermentation, and little or no aging in oak barrels. Emphasis on the preservation of aroma usually comes at the expense of alternate flavor and scent complexities. *See bouquet.*

Associated Vintners

In 1962, a group of amateur winemakers, dedicated to premium vinifera wines from Washington grapes, formed a corporation and became a bonded winery. This group of University of Washington college professors had bonded a commercial winery only to comply with legal restrictions on their amateur winemaking.

Later, led by psychology professor LLoyd Woodburne, and prompted by wine authority Leon Adams, and the dean of American winemakers, Andre Tchelistcheff, the group, in 1967, made their first commercial vintage. Washington's oldest, continuously operating, premium winery carries on its dedicated tradition today, under its new name, Columbia Winery.

BATF

Bureau of Alcohol, Tobacco and Firearms. A Federal regulatory agency.

Bainbridge Island

Puget Sound islands were site of some of Washington's earliest grape growing efforts. Today, Bainbridge Island is a focal point for western Washington winegrowing. The quantity is miniscule, but Muller-Thurgau, Madeleine Angevine, Siegerrebe, and other less common grape varieties show that fine wines are possible when cool climate grapes are matched to the right climate, and not overcropped.

Balcom and Moe

In 1927, the Balcom and Moe families formed a farming partnership. In 1971, Balcom and Moe planted the first commercial vinifera vineyard in a new viticultural area, just north of the city of Pasco. Washington's wine industry was not yet firmly established, and the first grapes had to be sold out of state to Oregon wineries. In 1985, Balcom and Moe produced the first vintage for their own winery, Quarry Lake.

Barrel

A container, usually made of oak, for fermenting and aging wine. (In the early days of the Oregon wine industry, and to a limited extent throughout the Northwest still today, many small wineries also purchased used, stainless steel, soft drink barrels as a cost-effective expedient for fermentation and storage containers).

Oak barrels are produced in a wide range of sizes and styles, but the typical wine barrel holds between fifty and sixty gallons of wine. Wood staves are bent into the barrel shape by fire (which also "toasts" the barrel), by steaming, or a combination of the two. The species of the oak, where it is grown, how it is cured, and how it is shaped into barrels, all play a part in the character of the barrel, and the flavors it imparts to the wine.

The oak flavors diminish with use. After many vintages, the barrel imparts little or no oak flavor, but still remains an excellent vessel for aging and mellowing wine—unless more pronounced oak flavors are required. Used barrels can be shaved, stripping away the spent surface and exposing a deeper layer of wood that still retains the oak flavors. *See oak.*

Barrel Fermentation

Certain white wines, typically Chardonnay, are sometimes fermented in individual oak barrels, in the manner of classic French white Burgundies, rather than in large stainless steel tanks. Proponents maintain that barrel fermented white wines are inherently more supple and complex.

Additionally, barrel fermented wines are exposed to slightly more oxygen, and because they are not in a reduced (starved for oxygen) state, the wines can safely be left on their lees (the sediment of pulp and dead yeast cells) without developing off flavors. Lees contact takes away some of the fruity taste of the wine, but offers richer, toasty flavors. *See lees.*

Berry Set

In late spring or early summer, the diminutive clusters of grape buds burst into flower. If the bloom is successful, grapes begin to form. Formation of the grapes from the delicate flowers is known as berry set. If the weather is cool and wet during bloom, the berries will not set as easily or uniformly.

Some grape varieties are more sensitive than others to weather conditions during bloom. Merlot is an example of a variety that needs ideal conditions to set well.

Western Oregon, particularly the Willamette Valley, has cool, wet springs. Some Oregon Merlot vineyards have failed to set a crop for several consecutive years. Although Merlot is not, in any case, destined to be a major Willamette Valley varietal, difficulties with berry set helps seal its fate. Conversely, Washington's Columbia Valley is known for its warm, dry climate, and Merlot is widely grown there. *See bloom, shot berries.*

Bloom

The period in late spring or early summer when the grape vines flower. Temperature and the seasonal change in day length determine the time of bloom. A critical time for the year's harvest, if the weather is too cool and rainy, the vine may fail to set a good crop.

Unlike most flowers, the tiny petals of the grape flower open at the base instead of the tip of the flower. These upside-down floral caps then fall away to facilitate pollination and formation of the grape berry. *See berry set, shot berries.*

Traditionally, if all the sugar is allowed to ferment completely, multiplying the Brix measurement of grapes or unfermented grape juice by .55 gives the approximate percentage of alcohol in the finished wine. For many reasons, including the efficiency of modern yeast strains, the conversion ratio is often slightly higher.

High Brix readings in grapes are often associated with quality and ripeness. This is a myth that dies slowly. Ripeness is determined not by sugar content, but by physiological maturity. In the Northwest, one of America's cooler winegrowing regions, physiological maturity occurs at lower Brix levels. Harvesting grapes beyond physiological ripeness, at higher Brix readings, diminishes the quality of the wine.

Brut

A descriptive term and label designation for dry sparkling wine. Brut is drier than sparkling wine labeled Extra Dry, but even the Brut designation has a degree of sweetness. Extra dry is a misnomer, and such wines are usually fairly sweet.

The carbonation and usually higher acidity of sparkling wines makes them taste less sweet. A completely dry sparkling wine would taste very tart and austere.

Bud Break

Grape vines loose their leaves and become dormant in winter. Bud break is the beginning of the new growth in spring, marking the beginning of the growing season—and a dangerous period for the vines.

Spring frosts threaten the tender new shoots, and an early bud break may mean an early bloom and less hospitable weather for the grape flowers. If the weather is too cool and rainy during bloom, a concern for western Oregon grape growers, the vines may not set a good crop.

Usually, a frost-free, early, bud break is welcome, bringing the promise of a longer growing season, but again, there are potential problems. Even in the cool Northwest, if the season is both early and unusually warm, grapes may ripen in overly hot conditions, and the wines will be unbalanced, with less acid, complexity, and finesse.

Bud break symbolizes the excitement, promise, and trauma that is so much a part of wine-growing. *See bloom, frost.*

Bulk Process

See Charmat Process.

Calapooya Mountains

Located south of the city of Eugene, halfway down western Oregon, the Calapooya Mountains form the southern boundary of Oregon's famed Willamette Valley.

Caliche

See hardpan.

Cane Training

A vine training system consisting of a vine trunk that forks at the top, forming very short, permanent arms. The arms are mere stubs, far shorter than the long permanent arms found on a cordon trained vine.

Each winter, the previous year's growth is pruned away, leaving (typically) only a single cane (mature shoot) for each of the vine's two stubby permanent arms. From the buds on the new canes, the coming year's new growth will emerge.

Cane training requires skilled labor and more work than cordon training, but it is far less sensitive to early spring weather conditions. If the early season weather is unfavorable or unpredictable, cane training is the method of choice for producing a reliable crop of grapes.

In the Northwest, Oregon, partly because of its cool and rainy spring climate, relies on cane training. In the major grape growing areas of Washington and Idaho, spring weather conditions are more favorable, and cordon training is the predominant method.

Many variations of cane training are possible. In Oregon, arc-cane training predominates. The canes are bent and tied to the vine trellis in an arc. The arced canes are longer, allowing more buds per vine, and potentially increasing the crop yield. Arc-cane training also promotes more consistent crop levels and more uniform vine growth. *See canopy management, cordon training, pruning, training.*

Canopy Management

The training and pruning of grape vines to achieve the desired amount of foliage, arrayed in a way that best benefits grape quality, yield, and vine health.

Warmer grape growing climates, such as most of California, traditionally emphasizes a broad leaf canopy to shade the grapes, protecting them from sunburning and preserving their acids. In the cooler grape growing climates of Europe and the Northwest, particularly western Oregon, a taller, more vertical canopy is desired to catch more of the sun, and to avoid shading the grapes and lower leaves.

Vertical, open canopies help reduce acidity in the grapes, increase sugars, speed ripening, and enhance grape quality. The number of vines per acre, training methods, and pruning methods all play a role in canopy management. *See cane training, cordon training, pruning, training, vine spacing.*

Cap

Red wines are fermented "on the skins." Unlike white wines, the skins and pulp are not removed prior to fermentation. As red wine ferments, the mass of skins and pulp is forced to the surface, forming a cap. Periodically, the cap must be broken up and remixed with the fermenting juice. Remixing the cap prevents spoilage and contamination, but it is also an important factor in extracting color and flavors from the grape. The frequency and method of remixing the cap affects character of the wine. *See maceration, pumping over, punching down.*

Carbon Dioxide

A gas given off during fermentation and usually allowed to escape into the atmosphere. Carbon dioxide is the source of the bubbles in sparkling wine.

Carbon River Valley

A minor western Washington grape growing area located south and east of the city of Tacoma.

Carbonic Maceration

A winemaking method for light, fruity, red wines that are drinkable within a month or two of the grape harvest. France's Beaujolais Nouveau, available on the market in the fall from the same year's harvest, is the best known carbonic maceration wine.

Grape berries are fermented whole, without crushing them, in an enclosed environment blanketed by carbon dioxide. Carbonic maceration wines are lightly colored with a fresh, fruity character and distinctive grapy fragrance and flavor. They are simple, but tasty wines.

The process is not an all or nothing proposition. Winemakers may include elements of carbonic maceration in their "more serious" red wines for a livelier, more fruity character. Grapes can be crushed after the carbonic maceration process has begun, whole grapes can be added to conventionally fermenting juice, and carbonic maceration wine can be blended with wine fermented in the conventional manner.

In the Northwest, Oregon winemakers have worked the most with carbonic maceration wines, usually making them from Pinot Noir. Release is rushed to coincide with the arrival by air of French Beaujolais Nouveau. Southwest Oregon is often the source for the grapes since they ripen earlier than Willamette Valley grapes.

Conventional wisdom dictates rapid consumption of carbonic maceration wines, but Oregon Pinot Noir Nouveau is often better after a few months in the bottle, and some take well to lengthier aging.

Cascade Mountains

A massive wall of volcanic mountains running north to south through Washington and Oregon. The mountains are a major factor in structuring and defining the winegrowing climates of the Northwest, affecting not only Washington and Oregon, but Idaho as well.

The influence is most dramatic for Washington's Columbia Valley, the Northwest's largest and most productive grape growing region. The Cascade Mountains block the onshore flow of marine air, casting a rain shadow that renders the Columbia Valley a near desert, and interplays with other climatic factors to make the Columbia Valley one of the most unique grape growing climates in the world.

Champagne

A sparkling wine from the Champagne district of France. Champagne is commonly, though incorrectly, used as a synonym for sparkling wine, no matter where it was made.

Champagne Process

See bottle fermented.

Chaptalization

The practice of adding sugar to the must before fermentation. Chaptalization is employed when the grapes have not achieved a sufficiently high sugar content. A widespread practice in the cool grape growing areas of Europe, chaptalization is seldom needed in warmer growing areas such as those of California and southern Europe.

Excessive chaptalization can unbalance a wine and create an artificial character. Abuses in France's Burgundy district are the most well known, and have given chaptalization a bad name. If used wisely and in moderation, however, chaptalization can be a positive quality factor.

In the Northwest, chaptalization is most common in the cool grape growing region of western Oregon. In the early years of the wine industry, Oregon winemakers rarely chaptalized Pinot Noir.

More recently, they have become more willing to chaptalize in cool vintage years—usually to the wine's benefit.

Contrary some notions, physiological ripeness of the grapes, and thus the flavor and quality of the wine, are not dependent on sugar content. Ideally, chaptalization merely augments the sugar content of already ripe grapes. *See ripeness.*

Charmat Process

A method for producing sparkling wines. Carbon dioxide bubbles are produced by a secondary fermentation in an enclosed tank rather than in the bottle. Carbon dioxide produced by the fermentation is trapped in the wine for later release in the form of bubbles. Typically, Charmat process sparkling wines are made from cheaper grapes and spend minimal time in contact with the sediment of yeast. Charmat process sparkling wines can be very good, but they rarely achieve the quality level of bottle fermented sparkling wines.

Few Charmat process sparkling wines are produced in the Northwest. The Charmat process requires a large monetary outlay for specialized equipment, and is practical only on a larger scale. Additionally, only the more expensive premium grape varieties are grown in the Northwest. Few cheap grapes are available for inexpensive Charmat process sparkling wines. *See bottle fermented.*

Chehalem Mountains

Located southwest of Portland, in Oregon's northern Willamette Valley, the hill-like Chehalem Mountains, are home to numerous vineyards and wineries.

Clearwater Valley

Idaho's Clearwater Valley was one of the Northwest's earliest grape growing regions. Except for experimental vineyards, the Clearwater Valley slipped into viticultural oblivion for many years.

Independent researcher Robert Wing's experimental vineyards and new commercial efforts suggest the beginnings of a viticultural reawakening in the valley. Much smaller and less open than the Snake River Valley, Idaho's major grape growing region, the Clearwater Valley brings promise of a new, premium, viticultural region.

Clone

A group of plants propagated asexually from a single plant. In the context of grape growing, clones are variations within a given grape variety.

A grape grower or researcher may notice that a particular grape vine ripens earlier, produces a larger crop, better tasting fruit, resists winter cold better, or any number of other criteria, and use cuttings from that vine to start other vines. In this way new clones are created.

Historically, this has been a casual and gradual process by the grape grower. In more modern times, systematic clonal selection programs are a routine part of viticultural research.

Some grape varieties are more genetically variable than others. Pinot Noir is, by far, one of the most variable, having hundreds of clonal variations.

In the Northwest, Oregon grape growers have an especially keen interest in clonal selection and testing. Many of Oregon's vines, notably, most of the Chardonnay vines, have come from clones developed in California, a grape growing region with a very different climate. Clones more specifically suited to the Oregon climate would further enhance the quality of Oregon wine. Oregon's focus on Pinot Noir also contributes to the interest in clonal selection and testing. *See Gamay, Pommard, Wadenswil.*

Cluster

Grape berries arrayed together on a stem structure to form a cluster. The clusters of premium vinifera wine grapes, as well as the berries themselves, are generally smaller than the clusters and berries of native American varieties and hybrids. Cluster size and shape also vary according to the specific grape variety. Chenin Blanc, for example, has large, long, cone-shaped clusters. Pinot Noir clusters are small and more cylindrical.

Cluster size is also dependent on growing climate and environment. The cluster size of California and Washington grapes are often larger than those of the same grape variety grown in Oregon's cooler climate.

Cluster Thinning

A method of limiting grape yield in a vineyard. High grape production may seem desirable, but if the yield is too high the grapes may not ripen properly, quality suffers, and the vines will be more susceptible to winter damage.

Vine pruning and training systems are the principal methods for controlling yield, but if too many grapes "set," cluster thinning will reduce the crop to desirable yields. Cluster thinning is accomplished by removing some of the grape clusters before they ripen. *See yield.*

Coast Range

A low-lying range of mountains running north to south along the coast of Oregon. The Coast Range is a key element in the western Oregon grape growing climate. The Coast Range moderates the flow of marine air into the inland valleys. Without the Coast Range, western Oregon would be too cool and wet for premium grape varieties. The moderating effect of the Coast Range helps create a Willamette Valley climate ideally suited to Pinot Noir, one of the world's most difficult and most rewarding grape varieties.

Cold Creek

Located south of the Columbia River, just after the river makes a ninety degree bend south of Mattawa, Cold Creek is the site of a 600 acre Chateau Ste. Michelle vineyard. The Cold Creek area is a very warm Columbia Valley growing site, well-suited to Cabernet Sauvignon.

Cold Stabilization

Wine is cold stabilized by lowering its temperature below freezing and precipitating potassium bitartrate crystals. White wines are frequently the recipients of cold stabilization because they are often chilled for several days or more prior to serving. If a wine is not cold stabilized, precipitation of tartrates can occur in the bottle.

The crystals are tasteless and harmless, but can cause concern on the part of the consumer who may think they are bits of glass, or that the wine is somehow defective (which it most certainly is not). *See tartrates.*

Color

The beautiful hues of wine are part of its aesthetic, but color also tells us about the wine. White wines range from a pale straw color to golden hues. Older white wines become more golden. Color may also vary according to wine type, although this frequently has as much to do with how the wine is made as to the grape it comes from.

Wines that are aged longer before release, aged in barrels, fermented at warmer temperatures, or finished with less sulfur dioxide (which strips away color) as a preservative are more darkly colored than wines treated oppositely. Partly because of these differences, Chardonnays are usually more darkly hued than Rieslings. If a wine is too dark for its type, it may be too old, or simply tired and oxidized before its time.

Red wines range from red to purple. Older red wines develop a brickish hue, observed most clearly at the edge of the glass. A young red wine with a brownish-brickish tinge is oxidized and old before its time.

Red wine grape varieties ·have different amounts and types of red pigments called anthocyanins. Pinot Noir, notably, has fewer anthocyanins than other red varieties. Pinot Noir wines are typically and naturally not as deeply colored as other red wines. An Oregon Pinot Noir (or any other Pinot Noir) should not be as darkly colored as a Cabernet Sauvignon.

Many factors affect red wine color. Wines from hot climates are less deeply colored. Vines and grapes exposed to more sunlight produce more deeply colored wines than shaded grapes grown under cloudy skies. Ample acidity and low pH form a wine's backbone and allow it to age. Young red wines are naturally more purplish, but a dull bluish-purple indicates wine that may be too low in acid or high in pH to age well. Higher acid, lower pH wines have more reddish than bluish hues.

Washington Cabernet Sauvignon grows in a very sunny climate, ripens under temperate conditions, and has ample fruit acidity. As expected from these conditions, the wines are typically an intense, brilliant, reddish-purple. *See acidity, anthocyanins, color, pH.*

Columbia Gorge

The Cascade Range, that massive wall of mountains running north to south through Washington and Oregon, is breached at only one point, where the great Columbia River cuts its way through the Cascades on its way to the Pacific Ocean. Along the narrow gorge, the radically different climates of the hot, dry, inland Columbia Valley and the moist, temperate, western, marine climate converge and collide. Winds race incessantly through the gorge, and major climatic differences occur within short distances.

Vineyard land is limited, but the full range of Northwest grape varieties can be grown in the gorge's numerous microclimates. Gewurztraminer from the gorge is particularly notable.

Columbia River

The famed Columbia River provides drainage for three-fourths of the entire Northwest region. Only southern Oregon is not part of the Columbia River system. The Columbia's irrigation water makes a rich agricultural industry possible in the near desert climate of the Columbia Valley.

Dammed and tamed for hydroelectric power, the Columbia is still an awesome presence. Its path through the Cascade Mountains is an important climatic influence on the inland grape growing regions. *See Columbia Gorge, Columbia Valley.*

Columbia Valley

The Northwest's largest winegrowing region, the vast Columbia Valley covers some 23,000 square miles, encompassing the Yakima Valley and Walla Walla Valley within its boundaries. Washington claims most of the land and nearly all the grape growing, but the Columbia Valley also extends into Oregon. In December of 1984, the BATF formally recognized 18,000 square miles of the Columbia Valley as an American viticultural area.

The Columbia Valley produces far more wine grapes than any other Northwest grape growing region. As a winegrowing climate, the Columbia Valley is unique. Located in the rain shadow of the towering Cascade Mountains, the Columbia Valley is a near desert. The growing season is relatively short and intense. At midsummer, during the height of the grape vine's vegetative period, the Columbia Valley averages two hours more sunlight than California's Napa Valley. As fall and the final grape ripening approach, day length in this more northerly growing climate rapidly decreases and the intense heat of the summer gives way to rapidly moderating temperatures.

Because the final ripening of the grapes does not take place in intense heat, the grape's volatile aromatics and flavoring components are preserved. In the cloudless, near desert climate, nighttime temperatures are relatively cool, even in the middle of summer. The nighttime coolness becomes even more exaggerated as fall and grape ripening approaches, further helping to preserve the grape acids and flavor components. Frosts and winter cold threaten the grape vines in some years, but improved viticultural practices have greatly reduced the potential for damage.

The Columbia Valley is the Northwest's most versatile winegrowing area. More varieties grow well in the Columbia Valley than in any other Northwest region. Grape growing climates within the Columbia Valley range from cool to very warm. Correspondingly, everything from Riesling to Cabernet Sauvignon can find excellent growing environments.

Cooper

A Craftsman who makes or repairs wooden barrels and tanks.

Cooperage

A general term for wooden wine barrels and tanks. Sometimes also refers to total wine production and storage capacity. *See barrel, oak.*

Cordon Training

A vine training system consisting of a vine trunk and permanent branches. In its most common form, known as bilateral cordon, two permanent arms (branches) split off the main trunk, shaping the vine in a capital "T." Cordon training has several advantages over other training systems (as well as some disadvantages). Cordon training requires less labor and less skill in the pruning process than cane training, another major vine training system. Cordon training is also adaptable to mechanical grape harvesting, and even mechanical pruning.

Each year, before new growth begins, all the prior year's growth is cut back to the permanent trunk and arms, with the exception of short spurs, left on the branches to begin the new year's growth. The spurs hold the buds that will become the new vine canes for the coming season. Some of these canes-to-be, in turn, will be pruned back to spurs the following year, as the cycle repeats.

When the first buds on the new cane, called basal buds, are forming in the spring, weather is critical. If weather conditions are unfavorable, the vine may not produce fruit in the subsequent growing season, a year away. In the Northwest, cordon training predominates in Washington and Idaho. Oregon, partly because of its cool and rainy spring climate, relies on cane training, a system not so dependent on early season weather conditions for a reliable crop. *See cane training, pruning, training.*

Crush

The period of time when the grapes are harvested, crushed, and made into wine. The term is also an apt metaphor for an exceptionally hectic time. For the winemaker, crush means many days with very little sleep. Because of the nature of their grape growing climates, the Washington and Idaho grape harvests are spread over a shorter time period, making crush all the more hectic—and all the more of a "crush."

Cuttings

Sections of vine cane used to propagate more grape vines. Because the Northwest is not troubled by the dreaded phylloxera louse, grape vines can be rooted directly from cuttings and do not require grafting on special phylloxera resistant rootstock.

Cuttings are taken during pruning and preserved for planting in the coming spring.

Cuvee

A French term with a variety of meanings. In the context of Champagne and other sparkling wines, the cuvee is the final blend of wines that may comprise different grape varieties, different vineyards, and different vintage years.

Day Length

An important factor in grape growing. Day length is mainly determined by the distance away from the equator. More northerly climates have longer summer days and more dramatic seasonal shifts as the days shorten and lengthen.

Grape vines need ample energy from the sun to produce a good crop of ripe grapes, but if conditions are too hot when the grapes are in their final ripening period, the grapes will loose too much acid, and many complex flavors will fail to develop or be burned away.

The total heat units of Oregon's Willamette Valley and California's Carneros region are similar, but the final ripening period is typically cooler in the more northerly Willamette Valley. Willamette Valley Pinot Noir typically ripens under more ideal conditions.

Washington's Columbia Valley receives two more hours of sunlight than California's Napa Valley during the height of the growing season. This intense period of sunlight and vine growth is followed by a rapid shift in day length and temperature for the final ripening of the grapes. The changes in day length, in combination with other climatic factors, is responsible for the Columbia Valley's productivity, high grape sugars, crisp acidity, and intense fruit flavors.

Decant

The process of transferring wine from the bottle into another vessel. White wines are generally not decanted. Red wines are often decanted for two principal reasons. Young red wines benefit from aeration, allowing them to open up in bouquet and taste and show more of what cellaring the wine might promise. Older red wines often throw a sediment in the bottle. Careful decanting of older red wines separates the wine from its sediment.

Disgorging

The process of removing the remaining yeast sediment from bottle fermented sparkling wines. After the riddling process has settled the yeast in the neck of the bottle, the yeast is frozen, the temporary bottle capsule is carefully removed, and the frozen plug of spent yeast is expelled. The wine is topped-up with more of the same wine, the dosage is added, and the sparkling wine receives its final corking. The disgorging process requires much care and skill. *See bottle fermented, dosage, riddling.*

Dosage

With rare exception, sparkling wines are finished with some residual sweetness, although the sweetness may not be readily apparent because of the wine's acidity and the sensory "drying" effect of the carbon dioxide bubbles.

Bottle fermented sparkling wines are sweetened with a dosage, a mixture of sugar, wine, and, in Champagne, brandy. The dosage is added after disgorging and just before the bottle receives its final corking. *See bottle fermented, disgorging.*

Dry

Dry is a variable term when applied to wine. In theory, a dry wine has no unfermented sugar remaining. In practice, many wines which are labeled "dry" actually have some residual sugar. Drinking dry wines is fashionable, but many prefer a touch of sweetness, particularly in white wines.

Producing traditionally fully dry wines with a touch of residual sugar is a current American winemaking trend. In the Northwest, Washington emphasizes this style in many of its Sauvignon Blancs and Semillons, combining a fresh fruity style and crisp acidity with a touch of residual sweetness. The style is very popular, but lovers of traditionally styled, fully dry wines may find them simplistic and cloying by the end of a meal.

Dundee Hills

The Red Hills of Dundee, in the northern Willamette Valley, is the site of Oregon's modern day Pinot Noir revolution. In the 1960s, Eyrie's David Lett came to Oregon to grow Pinot Noir. Lett established his vineyard in the red-soiled hills near the small town of Dundee.

Pinot Noir, Oregon's finest wine grape, is now grown throughout the Willamette Valley and western Oregon, but the Dundee Hills remain one of the state's prime Pinot Noir winegrowing areas. In 1987, Robert Drouhin of France's respected Burgundian wine firm, Joseph Drouhin, purchased nearly 100 acres of vineyard land in the Dundee Hills.

Enology

Also spelled oenology. The science and study of wine.

Eola Hills

A winegrowing area within Oregon's Willamette Valley, the Eola Hills rise up from the Willamette River near Salem and run northward for a short distance. Unlike most of the first Willamette Valley grape growing areas, the Eola Hills is located in the center of the valley, rather than on the valley's western edge.

Esters

Fruity, fragrant components of wine that come from the grape itself, from the action of yeast during fermentation, and from the interaction of alcohols and acids during the aging process. Some, like ethyl acetate, which smells like lacquer thinner, are undesirable. Others play important roles in the complex of flavors and scents that are intrinsic to fine wine.

Extra Dry

A descriptive term and label designation for sparkling wine. Extra Dry is a misnomer, and such wines are actually fairly sweet. *See Brut.*

Fan Training

An eastern european vine training system that was adopted by Washington grape growers in the early years of the industry. Winter freezing was considered a major threat to the wine industry. It was by no means certain that premium wine grapes could survive over an extended period of time in Washington's Columbia Valley. Fan training was viewed as the potential salvation for the industry—or, at least, added insurance.

A fan trained vine has not just one trunk, but three to five, fanning out from the base in the shape of a bush. In the original rendition of the system, new trunks were allowed to replace older trunks, so that none were more than three years old. Still young, the flexible trunks could be removed from the wire trellis and covered with soil for winter protection.

As vineyards grew larger, this labor intensive practice became impractical. Mature vines were left on the trellis, and soil was mounded up at the base of the trunks. Eventually, fan training was considered unnecessary for winter protection, and conventional bilateral cordon training became the norm.

New vineyards are very rarely fanned trained. The very few growers that fan train new vineyards do so for reasons other than winter protection. The sight of a fan trained vine is a striking reminder that the success of the Washington wine industry, now regarded so matter of factly, was a very tenuous proposition not so long ago. *See cordon training, training.*

Fermentation

The action of yeast on the sugar and nutrients in grape juice, creating alcohol, carbon dioxide, and a multitude of flavor and aroma compounds. Technically speaking, fermentation is the transformation of an organic substance by an agent. Yeast/alcohol fermentations are only one type.

Malolactic fermentation is another type of fermentation associated with most red wines and some white wines. It is a bacterial fermentation that converts malic acid into lactic acid, reducing the total acidity of the wine and contributing its own set of flavor and aroma compounds. *See malolactic fermentation.*

Fermentation Temperature

The temperature of fermentation affects the taste and style of wine. Roughly 95 degrees fahrenheit is considered the upper maximum. Some winemakers allow red wines to reach this fermentation temperature, but beyond this, volatile acidity (acetic acid) and oxidation become critical concerns.

The lower fermentation temperature limit is only a few degrees above freezing. Very low fermentation temperatures require many months to complete. Stuck fermentations are also more of a risk with low fermentation temperatures. Restarting a stuck fermentation is usually difficult, and the wine is more susceptible to contamination by other organisms.

In practice, most wine is fermented at between 45 and 90 degrees. Higher temperatures extract more from the grape at the loss of some of the fresh fruity flavors. Lower fermentation temperatures preserve the fruitiness of the grape at the loss of richer, more complex flavors.

Red wines are typically allowed to peak at higher temperatures. White wines are usually fermented at lower temperatures. In the Northwest, wines in which the fresh fruity characteristics are most desired, such as Riesling and Chenin Blanc, are typically fermented at the coolest temperatures, Chardonnay a bit warmer, and Cabernet Sauvignon, Pinot Noir, and other red wines toward the upper temperature limit.

Filtering

A method of clarifying wine by passing it through a medium that traps the suspended matter. The filter medium may be very coarse to trap only the largest particles, or extremely fine to trap yeast cells and other microorganisms. Wines with residual sugar are often sterile filtered to prevent the wine from refermenting in the bottle.

Wines are not always filtered. A tight filtration can strip away flavor elements, though a proper coarse filtration does little harm. Winemaking, as with many other things, is a trade-off, balancing benefit and loss for the the best overall result. *See fining.*

Fining

A method of clarifying wine by mixing a fining agent with the wine. The fining agent combines with the suspended matter and settles out of the wine. Egg whites are a traditional and gentle fining agent. Others include gelatin, casein, and bentonite.

Fining agents are chosen for their particular attributes, depending on the need. Some can strip away character and, if used in excess, contribute off and intrusive flavors to the wine. *See filtering.*

Finish

The wine's aftertaste. Great wines typically have a complex, enduring finish. Young wines often have a short finish, simply because of their youth.

Free Run

The juice that comes from the grapes after crushing, but before pressing, or after only a light pressing. It is the juice that runs freely from the crushed grapes, hence the name. Free run juice is sweeter and less astringent than juice from a heavy pressing. Wine is usually made from a combination of free run and press juice. *See press wine.*

French-American Hybrid

A crossing of premium wine grape varieties of the *Vitis vinifera* species with native American species such as *Vitis labrusca* or *Vitis riparia*. Most of the French-American hybrids that find their way into commercial use are the end products of a long series of crossings and recrossings. Seyval Blanc, Campbell Early, Island Belle, Marechal Foch, and Baco Noir are a few examples of the many French-American varieties.

With occasional exception, wines produced from French-American hybrids are inferior to wines produced from the classic wine grape species, *Vitis vinifera*, whose varieties include Cabernet Sauvignon, Chardonnay, Pinot Noir, etc.

French-American varieties are highly resistant to diseases and winter cold. They can be grown in places where the growing season is too cool or the environmental factors too harsh for vinifera varieties to prosper. French-American hybrids played a role in the early days of the Northwest wine industry, but they have been virtually abandoned in favor of the vinifera varieties. A few Northwest wineries produce French-American hybrids as unique speciality wines.

Frost

Frosts threaten the vines in spring and fall. In the spring, frost can damage the tender new shoots, and greatly reduce the year's harvest. In the fall, an early frost can damage the foliage, preventing or greatly slowing the ripening process and weakening the vines against the winter cold.

For most of western Oregon's Willamette Valley vineyards, frost is seldom a problem. In southern Oregon, Idaho's Snake River Valley, and, especially in Washington's Columbia Valley, severe frosts are a major threat in some years.

Gamay

The name may refer to the grape of French Beaujolais, or one of the misnamed grape varieties grown in America that have been mistaken for the grape of Beaujolais, or a clone Pinot Noir.

A few Oregon winegrowers are experimenting with the true Gamay of France's Beaujolais region, Gamay Noir au Jus Blanc. The grape shows promise as a relatively high producing variety, offering a quality, moderately priced wine for the consumer. Widespread commercial availability is years away, however.

Gamay also refers to a clone of Pinot Noir. The Gamay clone is out of favor in Oregon, having the reputation for producing big berries and lightly flavored, lightly colored, overly acidic wine. The reputation is not entirely deserved. Cropped moderately and planted on a good growing site, the Gamay clone produces finely flavored wines with good fruit, and an acid structure sometimes lacking in Oregon Pinot Noir.

The Gamay clone ages well, developing complex flavors and sometimes deepening in color. A few of Oregon's top Pinot Noir winemakers, Amity's Myron Redford and Eyrie's David Lett among them, actively seek the Gamay clone as an integral component of their Pinot Noir. *See clone, Pommard, Wadenswil.*

Geneva Double Curtain

A system of vine pruning and training developed for Concord grapes by Dr. Nelson Shaulis and his colleagues at the Geneva research station in New York. The tall vine trunks and permanent arms are arranged so that the new growth hangs downward. The foliage runs down two wires, spread apart in the row in a double curtain, exposing more of the vine to sunlight.

Although best suited for the droopier Concord vines, the practice has been adapted to premium vinifera wine grape vines. Though not a mainstream practice, several new Oregon vineyards are trained to this system. The system addresses some of Oregon's winegrowing needs, including more direct sunlight to the vine, and increased grape yield without a reduction in quality. *See training.*

Grape

The fruit of the vine, and the fruit source for all the world's great wines. More specifically, the grape species *Vitis vinifera* is the the source for the world's finest wines. Cabernet Sauvignon, Pinot Noir, Chardonnay, and Riesling are examples of the literally thousands of varieties of *Vitis vinifera. See Vitis vinifera.*

Harden Off

Grape vines enter a period of dormancy during the winter months. In Washington and Idaho, winters can be severe, and the health and survival of the grape vines is dependent on the vines preparation for winter. Irrigation is halted in late summer so that the vines will reduce their vegetative growth and begin to harden off early in the fall, storing carbohydrate reserves that will act as a viticultural antifreeze for the winter months.

Hardpan

Also called caliche, it is a hard crust of calcium carbonate that often forms in the soils of arid regions. In many areas of Washington's Columbia Valley, the state's principal grape growing region, the vineyard soils have an underlying layer of hardpan. The hardpan inhibits or prevents the penetration of moisture and vine roots.

The hardpan's threat to the vines became clear in the disastrous freeze of the 1978—79 winter. In some vineyards, vigorous, well-established vines were easily killed by the freeze. Investigation showed that the vine roots had not penetrated deeply into the soil, but spread laterally near the surface after running against the hardpan. The freezing temperatures simply penetrated the surface soil and killed the unprotected vines.

There were many reasons for the severe winter damage, but the layer of hardpan was a significant one of them. To prevent a repeat of the disaster, vineyard soils are "ripped" before planting, breaking up the layer of hardpan.

Heat Units

The American wine industry's primary analytical tool for evaluating winegrowing climates is the heat summation method formulated at the University of California at Davis. When comparisons are drawn between a new winegrowing region and European growing climates, heat unit measurements inevitably become part of the discussion.

Comparative climatic evaluation is obtained by totaling the number of degrees the average daily temperature is above 50 degrees for all the days of the growing season. If, for example, the average daily temperature is 65 degrees, 15 heat units (65 - 50 = 15) would be added to the year's total. The mean of the day's high and low temperatures is generally considered the average daily temperature. The yearly totals are divided into five summation ranges or "regions" for climate comparison.

Though perhaps the single most useful measurement of a growing climate, heat summation is a much rougher guide than popularly presumed. Especially outside of California, particularly in the Northwest, its limitations are increasingly apparent. Each of the five heat summation regions has a broad range, lumping together, in the cooler regions, climatic differences that are critical to the performance of premium grape varieties.

A daily high and low of 72 degrees and 68 degrees has the same heat unit value as a daily high and low of 100 degrees and 40 degrees, yet such temperatures during grape ripening would have considerably different implications, as would a daily high of 90 degrees maintained for one hour versus a 90 degree high maintained for 10 hours.

The similarity of heat units is admittedly one of the most important keys in determining if a region can produce premium wines, yet many regions in America have heat units similar to those of European growing climates, but are completely unsuitable for grape growing.

Among other basic climatic requirements is the necessity for winters cool enough to allow the vines to become dormant, but not cold enough to kill them, and the necessity for a growing season long enough to ripen the grapes. Beyond the basic factors, countless variables come into play. Day length (latitude), duration and range of maximum and minimum temperatures, nighttime cooling, cloud cover, soil reflectance, and heat during grape ripening versus heat during the vegetative period are a few of the many considerations contributing to the character of the grape, and ultimately, the quality of the wine.

Heat unit measurements as quality indicators are most useful and reliable when these other factors are held relatively constant, which is to say, within a narrowly delimited climatic and geographic region. Clearly, however, the world's winegrowing climates and geography vary widely, and these other factors are always in play.

European viticulture is generally more attentive to these other factors, but the wine industry is far from any comprehensive system of analysis, and particularly in the Northwest, where growing conditions vary significantly, these other factors define key viticultural differences—and remain largely unmeasured.

Hedging

During the course of the growing season, grape vines send out numerous lateral shoots. In warm winegrowing climates, a broad leaf canopy helps retain acidity and protect the grapes from sunburning. In cooler climates, it is desirable to expose as much of the vine to sunlight as possible. Depending on the training and trellising system, the grape grower may choose to hedge the vines, going down the vine rows to trim back excess foliage hanging into the row. In the Northwest, hedging is most common in western Oregon. *See pruning, training.*

Horse Heaven Hills

Part of the southern boundary of Washington's Yakima Valley.

Hybrid

The result of crossing two different genera, species, or varieties. In the context of wine, hybrid almost always refers to an interspecific hybrid, the crossing of two species of grapes, *Vitis vinifera* and one of the native American species. These are called French hybrids, or French-American hybrids, and are often crossed again and again with themselves to produce a seemingly endless number of varieties. *See French-American hybrid, Vitis vinifera.*

Hydrogen Sulfide

A wine defect with an odor of rotten eggs. A by-product of the fermentation process involving the interaction of yeast and sulfur compounds, and also caused by decaying yeast cells after the fermentation process has finished. Although easily correctable by the winemaker, hydrogen sulfide sometimes finds its way into the bottle. If not corrected early in the winemaking process, other, more stubborn, off odors may be formed. *See mercaptans.*

Ice Wine

An American term derived from the German *eiswein.* Ice wine is a sweet dessert wine made from frozen grapes. It is possible to "cheat" and freeze grapes artificially, but legitimate ice wines are made from grapes ripening long on the vine, late into fall—or even winter. Ice wines have been harvested as late as the January following the vintage.

Ice wines are made by quickly harvesting grapes frozen on the vine, sometimes in the dark of night before sunrise, rushing them to the winery, and crushing them before they thaw. Sugar solutions resist freezing, so the sweetest grapes, and the sweetest part of each grape, yield the juice. The less sweet grapes and the less sweet part of each grape remains frozen. The best ice wines are richly sweet, balanced, and concentrated. Botrytis helps quality, but it is not an intrinsic element in ice wine.

Making ice wine is risky business. If the weather is not cooperative, the grapes may not be harvestable, or they may not be entirely suitable for either table wine or a sweet ice wine. Oregon, Washington, and Idaho have all produced ice wines. Washington lends itself especially well to them because of the Columbia Valley's dry, cold, fall climate. Riesling is the classic ice wine grape, but other varieties, such as Gewurztraminer, make fine ice wine as well.

Idaho

Idaho wine grape growing dates back to the late 1860s, in the Clearwater Valley, in the northwestern part of the state. After a long dormancy, the industry began anew in the 1970s. Now, approximately 1,000 acres are planted to wine grapes, virtually all in the Snake River Valley, in the southwestern part of the state. Riesling and Chardonnay are the major grape varieties. Other grape varieties include Gewurztraminer and Chenin Blanc. The Clearwater Valley is also beginning to reawaken, experimental vineyards generating interest in small scale commercial winegrowing ventures.

Illinois Valley

One of the warmest grape growing areas in western Oregon, only slightly cooler than the nearby Applegate Valley. Located near the California border, the Illinois Valley has a shorter, more intense growing season than other parts of western Oregon. Unlike the the Willamette Valley to the north, the threat of frosts is routine. Warmer climate grapes like Cabernet Sauvignon and Semillon are well-suited to the Illinois Valley.

Interspecific Hybrid

The result of genetically crossing two different species. In the context of wine, French-American hybrids such as Marechal Foch, Campbell Early, and Island Belle are examples of interspecific hybrids. *See French-American hybrid, hybrid.*

Irrigated Agricultural Research and Extension Center

Located near the town of Prosser, in the Yakima Valley, Washington State University's extension station was and is the center for Washington state's winegrowing research. The work of pioneer researcher Dr. Walter Clore began in the 1930s, but decades would pass before the consumer and business climate was ripe for a premium wine industry.

Irrigation

Grape vines can survive and grow in very hot, arid environments without irrigation, but irrigation is often desirable. Irrigation has many secondary benefits, but principally, irrigation helps new vines produce grapes sooner, and allows older vines to produce more grapes.

In Washington's Columbia Valley and Idaho's Snake River Valley, the states' major grape growing regions, nearly all vineyards are irrigated. Vineyards in Oregon's major grape growing area, the relatively moist Willamette Valley, are rarely irrigated. In the drier climate of southwest Oregon, irrigation again becomes more of a necessity. In wet western Washington, irrigation would be more than redundant.

Irrigation has some special implications for Washington's Columbia Valley and Idaho's Snake River Valley. Since there is so little rainfall in these regions, irrigated "rainfall" can be controlled at will.

Excessive irrigation produces very large crops in these regions, but at the expense of grape quality—and, at the risk of winter damage to the weakened vine. Good grape growing practices call for moderate irrigation, and for ending irrigation in late summer. An early end to irrigation prompts the vines to begin building ample carbohydrate reserves for winter and to rapidly enter into a protective dormancy.

Klamath Mountains

Geologically distinct from the Coast Range, the Klamath Mountains, in the southwestern corner of Oregon, shelter Oregon's southwestern grape growing regions from Pacific marine air. The many small Klamath valleys are home to scattered vineyards.

Labrusca

See *Vitis labrusca*.

Lactic Acid

A minor acid in wines that have only undergone a yeast fermentation, lactic acid is a much more major presence in wines that have also undergone the bacterial malolactic fermentation. In a malolactic fermentation, malic acid is converted to the less strong lactic acid.

Lactic acid is an important component in classic red wines as well as many of the classic white wines, such as French white Burgundy from the Chardonnay grape. Grapes grown in cool climates have a higher ratio of malic acid, and thus, if the cool climate wines are put through a malolactic fermentation, have a higher ratio of lactic acid than wines made from warmer climate grapes. The cool climate of the Northwest winegrowing states fits this pattern. *See malolactic fermentation.*

Lees

The sediment of yeast cells and pulp that settles out of a wine after fermentation. Before bottling, the wine must be removed from the lees, a process known as racking.

Rotten egg (hydrogen sulfide) and skunky (mercaptan) smells can form if a wine is allowed to remain on the lees too long. These off flavors form when the wine is in a "reduced" (starved for oxygen) state, a particular concern when the wine has been fermented and kept in enclosed tanks.

Lees can also contribute rich, complex, toasty flavors to wine. Wine that has been fermented and aged in oak barrels usually has sufficient oxygen to prevent the off flavors from forming. Certain wines, typically Chardonnays, are sometimes left on the lees for as much as a year to gain a richer, toasty character.

Winemaking practices differ greatly. Most (but not all) Washington winemakers favor fermenting Chardonnay in stainless steel tanks and minimizing the exposure to lees. At the other end of the winemaking spectrum, most (but not all) Oregon winemakers favor barrel fermented Chardonnays and lees contact. *See barrel fermentation.*

Limousin Oak

A type of French oak widely used for barrel aging wines. At one time the predominant French oak in American winemaking, especially for barrel aging Chardonnays, Limousin is losing ground to other French oaks.

Because of its loose grain structure, Limousin oak imparts its aggressive flavors more quickly than the tighter grained French oaks. Limousin barrels are often the choice for wines requiring a great deal of oak character, or requiring oak character quickly, such as Chardonnays made in a heavily oaked style. As with all oak barrels, the oak character diminishes with use.

Linalool

A flavor and aroma component largely responsible for the distinctive character of muscat grapes and wines. Linalool is present in riper Riesling grapes. Many Washington Rieslings, as well as some from Idaho, frequently have muscat-like elements. This is particularly true in the late harvest renditions. The muscat element is less present in Oregon Rieslings.

The greatest contrast exists between German Rieslings and California Rieslings. A large part of the California Riesling character, the linalool-muscat component, is rare in German Rieslings.

Maceration

Grape skins and pulp are not removed when red wines are fermented. Color, tannin, and many flavor constituents come from the breakdown of skins and pulp during fermentation. This process is called maceration.

Maceration, and thus flavor extraction, is assisted by periodically mixing and squeezing the skins and pulp, by fermenting at higher temperatures, and by leaving the skins and pulp in the fermenting juice for a longer time before removing them. *See cap, fermentation temperature, pumping over, punching down.*

Maderization

The oxidation of wine. Maderization turns wine brownish and gives it a flat, dull taste. Unprotected by tannins and pigments, white wines are more susceptible to maderization than red wines. Maderization is usually associated with the type of oxidation and flavors that comes from excess heat in storing or aging the wine, and a dull caramelized character.

Magnum

A larger bottle size. The equivalent of two regular size wine bottles.

Malic Acid

Along with tartaric acid, malic acid is one of the major acids in grapes. Because heat and sunlight respire (diminish) malic acid far more readily than tartaric acid, grapes grown in cool climates have a higher ratio of malic acid to tartaric acid—as well as more acid overall. Winemakers may choose to convert malic acid into a weaker and differently flavored acid, lactic acid. *See malolactic fermentation.*

Malolactic Fermentation

Sometimes abbreviated "ML," it is a bacterial action that converts malic acid into the less acidic lactic acid. Because it begins after the yeast fermentation that converts sugar to alcohol, it is sometimes referred to as the secondary fermentation. Malolactic fermentation not only reduces acid, it changes the character of the wine as well, taking away some of the fruit flavors while adding flavor complexities of its own. Ironically, if a wine is too acid, the bacterial fermentation will not take place.

Malolactic fermentation is almost always desirable in red wines. For white wines, it is a matter of grape variety, growing climate, and style. Floral/fruity varieties such as Riesling are rarely put through malolactic fermentation, taste odd if they have gone through it, and are usually too high in acid for the bacteria to work even if it were desired. Chardonnay is the white variety most often put through ML, though practices vary widely. Virtually all French white Burgundies go through ML.

Oregon Chardonnay, typically high in acid, is almost always put through ML. The ML is a heavy one, and is partly responsible for the full yet soft and delicate character that typifies Oregon Chardonnay.

Though Washington Chardonnay can be relatively high in acid, most Washington winemakers prefer a style of Chardonnay that emphasizes more of the fruit of the grape, and thus avoid ML in their Chardonnays. Washington's malolactic Chardonnays, however, are usually the best the state produces.

Malolactic fermentations in California, though still significant, have much less of an effect. Not only are grapes grown in warmer climates lower in acid, they have a lower ratio of malic acid to other acids.

Traditionally, malolactic fermentation was not encouraged until after the alcohol fermentation had finished and the wine was in the barrel. Now, ML is often begun sometime during the alcohol fermentation, a practice that many believe yields a cleaner, less troublesome wine. ML occurring after the wine is bottled is undesirable, giving a spritzy character and unpleasant smell and taste.

Like yeasts, ML cultures have differing characteristics. The strains vary according to vigor, flavor contributions, cleanness of fermentation, and adaptation to higher acid levels or lower temperatures. *See acid and pH.*

May Wine

Traditionally a German white wine flavored with woodruff, and often served with strawberries floating in it. Although not common in the Northwest, wineries in both Washington and Oregon produce their own versions of May wine, usually based on Riesling, or occasionally, Chenin Blanc.

Mead

A drink made from fermented honey. Few meads are produced in the Northwest. They can be quite good drinks, different than grape wines, but with their own set of interesting and complex attributes.

Mercaptan

A wine defect. Mercaptans have an unpleasant skunky odor. If hydrogen sulfide, another wine defect, is not prevented or removed quickly from a wine, the hydrogen sulfide may be converted into mercaptans, a defect more difficult to correct. *See hydrogen sulfide.*

Methode Champenoise

See bottle fermented.

Microclimate

A term referring to a climate with specific characteristics within a larger, more generally defined climate. The term is elastic in scope, and is sometimes used to refer to the environment as small as that encompassed by a single grapevine (a more recent, technical usage of the term), or as large as an entire valley. More typically, a microclimate refers to a portion of a vineyard, a vineyard, or a contiguous grape growing site sharing climatic factors distinguishing it from a larger grape growing area.

A small ridge or crest running through a vineyard that catches more sun and causes the grapes to ripen more or sooner would be an example of a microclimate. The Red Willow vineyard, on a pronounced slope at the far northwestern end of the Yakima Valley, is an example of a vineyard microclimate. The collection of vineyards on Red Mountain, at the warm southeastern end of the Yakima Valley, where the river bends sharply before entering the Columbia River, is an example of a microclimate encompassing several vineyards. The Dundee Hills in Oregon's northern Willamette Valley is another such example.

Must

The juice of the grape before it has completed fermentation and been turned into wine.

Musty

An undesirable smell and taste that has a dank mold-like quality. The character can come from wooden barrels that have not been properly maintained, or, conversely, from excess sulfur dioxide, a compound used in various forms to protect wine and barrels.

Mute

Unfermented or partially fermented grape juice added to table wine or aperitif wine as a sweetener. In the case of aperitifs, brandy or other high proof alcohol is added to the grape juice to prevent fermentation and to raise the alcohol level of the aperitif. *See sweet reserve.*

Nawico

Immediately following Repeal of Prohibition, two wineries, Nawico and Pommerelle, began producing wines from hybrids and native American grape varieties. In 1954, the two wineries merged to form American Winegrowers. For the the 1967 vintage, American Winegrowers released a line of vinifera wines under a new premium label, Ste. Michelle.

Netting

In some grape growing regions, birds pose a major threat to the grape harvest. Before grapes reach sugar levels high enough for harvest, they are already attractive food for birds. Many methods are employed to protect the grapes. Netting is one of the most effective, though expensive and requiring more labor than other methods.

In the Northwest, Oregon vineyards are most at risk from bird damage. Migrating flocks of Canadian robins can and have virtually wiped out an entire year's grape harvest in some vineyards. Robins are persistent and do not frighten easily. Netting the vineyard rows before the grapes ripen enough to attract the robins presents a physical barrier which simply denies them access to the grapes.

Nevers Oak

A French oak widely used for barrel aging both red and white wines. Often the French oak of choice for aging Cabernet Sauvignon.

Noble Rot

A term for the mold *Botrytis cinerea* when it is present in a beneficial form. The mold is responsible for some of the world's great sweet wines. *See Botrytis cinerea.*

Nooksack Valley

Near the Canadian border, in northwest Washington, the Nooksack River flows from the slopes of Mt. Baker, one of the Northwest's towering, snow-covered, volcanic cones. A relatively warm growing area in western Washington's very cool, rainy climate, the Nooksack Valley is one of the focal points for western Washington winegrowing. The acreage devoted to grape growing is miniscule, but Madeleine Angevine and other very cool climate grape varieties demonstrate the interest and viability of western Washington winegrowing.

Nouveau

Literally, new wine, usually made by the carbonic maceration fermentation method in a very grapy, fruity style for consumption soon after the harvest. *See carbonic maceration.*

Oak

Nearly all red wines and many white wines are aged in oak barrels. White wines, particularly Chardonnay, are also sometimes fermented in oak barrels, a practice, in the Northwest, most common in Oregon. In the winemaking process, oak should augment a wine's natural character, without competing with the wine or overwhelming it.

Some wines never see oak. Northwest Riesling is a typical example of an oakless wine, a wine made in a style that emphasizes the fresh fruity character of the grape rather than the complexities that would be enhanced by aging in oak barrels.

The character of oak is most closely described as vanilla-like, but its character is much more complex, and varies widely, depending on the species of oak, where it is grown, how the wood is dried, and how it is bent and made into barrels. Some of the more common oaks used for wine barrels are listed separately in this book. *See Allier, American, Limousin, Nevers, and Oregon oaks.*

Oechsle

A German scale for measuring the amount of unfermented sugar in grapes or grape juice. In America, Brix is the common scale of measure. *See Brix.*

Oenology

See enology.

Oregon

The Oregon wine industry dates back to the 1800s. After a long period of dormancy, premium winegrowing emerged again in the 1960s, in the Umpqua and Willamette Valleys of western Oregon. Now, some 5,000 acres are in vine.

The Willamette Valley is Oregon's largest and most productive winegrowing region. Other grape growing areas include the Umpqua Valley, Applegate Valley, and Illinois Valley in western Oregon, the Columbia Gorge at the state's northern border, as well as the the newer and much warmer winegrowing areas east of the Cascade Mountains in the Columbia and Walla Walla Valleys.

Pinot Noir, Chardonnay, and Riesling are the major grape varieties. Pinot Noir is clearly Oregon's star grape. A great but fickle grape, Pinot Noir rarely does well outside of France's Burgundy district. Oregon's Willamette Valley is one of the rare winegrowing regions in the world producing exceptional Pinot Noir.

Oregon Oak

A native Northwest oak species, *Quercus garryana*, has caught the interest of several Northwest winemakers. Oregon oak seemed a natural and logical feature of the regional wine style, but problems obtaining, curing, and coopering suitable wood have kept Oregon oak more of an interesting promise than an established constituent of Northwest wine.

Organoleptic

A sensory, as opposed to a chemical, evaluation of wine. Chemical analysis is an important tool in making and evaluating wine. But ultimately, an organoleptic assessment is the final arbiter. How a wine smells and tastes and the pleasure it offers are what wine and its enjoyment are all about.

Overcropping

Harvesting an excessive crop of grapes. Grapes from overcropped vines usually lack fruit intensity. The grapes ripen later, and less well. In Washington, vines weakened from overcropping are more susceptible to winter damage.

Oxidation

A wine flaw that turns wine brownish and gives it a flat, dull taste. Unprotected by tannins and pigments, white wines oxidize more easily than red wines.

In actuality, controlled oxidation is desirable for most wines. Wine that has been starved for oxygen during the winemaking and aging process will develop fewer complex flavors and may be more at risk for development of off flavors. This is one reason why wines made in a fresh fruity style usually do not age particularly well.

Pacific Ocean

The western border of Washington and Oregon. Marine air from the Pacific Ocean plays a key role in Northwest winegrowing climates. The full impact of Pacific marine air would render the Northwest too cold and too rainy, and useless as a winegrowing climate, but modified by mountain ranges and landforms, the tempering effect of Pacific marine air helps create ideal winegrowing climates. Even Idaho's Snake River Valley, several hundred miles inland, is affected by marine air traveling the pathways of the Columbia and Snake Rivers. Without the Pacific marine influence, the climate would be too harsh for wine grapes.

Pacific Ring of Fire

A ring of extinct, dormant, and active volcanoes embracing the Pacific Ocean. The Northwest's dramatic topology has been shaped by millions of years of volcanic tumult. The Northwest's topology, in turn, shapes the winegrowing climate. The towering Cascade Mountain Range, Oregon's Coast Range, the massive lava flows across the vast Columbia Valley, the uplift of the Willamette Valley out of the ocean, and on and on, are end products of the tumultuous volcanic workings. In conjunction with the northerly latitude and the Pacific marine air, they define and shape the Northwest winegrowing climate.

Pasco Basin

Floodwaters from an ancient glacial lake dammed up behind the narrow Wallula Gap near what is today the Tri-Cities area of Washington's Columbia Valley. The sediment of the briefly stilled floodwaters settled out to form the soils for the nearly slopeless vineyards in the Pasco Basin.

Paterson Ridge

Site of the Northwest's largest vineyard, the 1,800 acres of vines surround the Columbia Crest winery on several sides. Paterson Ridge is located near the town of Paterson, Washington, along the lower slopes of the Horse Heaven Hills, near the Columbia River.

Perry

A term for pear wine or cider. Several Northwest wineries make or have made pear wine, sometimes labeling it perry.

pH

One of the ways of measuring and characterizing the acidity of a solution. Absolutely pure water has a pH of 7.0 Acidic solutions, such as wine, orange juice, and vinegar, have pHs of less than 7.0. Basic solutions, such as household ammonia, have pHs of more than 7.0

Wines usually have pHs ranging from 3 to 4. Generally speaking, the pH of wine should ideally be no higher than 3.6. Wines with lower pH are more chemically and biologically stable, develop better flavors with age, age longer, and have better color.

A solution of a weak acid and a salt of the acid is said to be a buffer solution. Tartaric acid and potassium bitartrate is a common example in wine. The degree of buffering affects how much a solution's pH will change with the addition of an acid or base.

What contributes to buffering and high pH in wine? Overcropping, excessive vegetative vine growth, excessive shading of the fruit, overly warm growing climate, overripe grapes, wide vine spacing, and excessive fertilization are among the many factors contributing to buffering and high pH.

In recent years, winemakers have come to better understand the importance of low pH in quality wine, but a few winemakers persist in the belief that high alcohol and tannin are more important factors in wine aging. Those who have held this position, and have had the opportunity to make wine over a period of years, can now observe the importance of low pH, as their high pH wines brown and fall apart.

High pH wines have a softer fuller taste that some wine drinkers find appealing, but such wines lack the clarity of voice of low pH wines, and fail to develop well in the bottle. *See acidity and total acidity.*

Phylloxera

A plant louse that devastated European vineyards in the late 1800s. American vines were the probable cause of the devastation, and also the cure. Phylloxera is indigenous to native American grape vines, but not particularly harmful to them. The classic vinifera grape varieties, however, are extremely susceptible to phylloxera. California vinifera vineyards became infected with the louse, as were European vineyards, which were probably infected by vines sent from America.

Countless methods were employed to stop the devastation. Ultimately, only two were successful. Hybrid crosses of classic vinifera varieties with native American varieties were resistant to the dreaded phylloxera. The quality of the wine from these French-American hybrids, however, ranges from reasonably good to very poor.

The second solution, and the one that saved the great European vineyards as well as the California vineyards, was to graft the classic vinifera varieties onto native American rootstocks. Today, most European and California vineyards are planted to these grafted vines.

The Northwest, so far, has been more fortunate. Virtually all Northwest vinifera vines are planted on their own rootstocks. Phylloxera may eventually spread to the Northwest, but the major winegrowing areas of Washington and Idaho have an added measure of protection with their sandy soils and environmental conditions hostile to the phylloxera louse.

It is said that ungrafted vines live longer and produce better grapes, and thus better wines. Others claim there is no substantive difference in quality. Any differences are probably minimal. Ungrafted vines do offer one clear advantage. They are more easily and quickly propagated.

Pips

Grape seeds. If the pips are damaged during grape crushing or pressing, they will add a bitterness to the wine.

Plate Tectonics

See tectonic plates.

Pommard

A clone of Pinot Noir. Pommard is the most widely planted Pinot Noir clone in Oregon. The other predominant clone, Wadenswil, is regarded as slightly more perfumed, but not quite as intensely flavored. The distinction has some merit, but the vineyard site, grape growing practices, and winemaking style have a far greater effect on the wine than clonal distinctions. Some vineyards have both clones, with the idea that a blend of the two will produce the best, most complex wine. *See clone, Wadenswil, Gamay.*

Pommerelle

Immediately following Repeal of Prohibition, two wineries, Pommerelle and Nawico, began producing wines from hybrids and native American grape varieties. In 1954, the two wineries merged to form American Winegrowers. For the the 1967 vintage, American Winegrowers released a line of vinifera wines under a new premium label, Ste. Michelle.

Port

A sweet, red, dessert wine, true port originates in the upper Douro Valley of Portugal. Many countries make a port-like wine labeled port. Some of these New World ports resemble port only in sweetness and high alcohol. Others come much closer to the quality level of the Portuguese product. Port is made by stopping fermentation very early, then fortifying with brandy to the desired alcohol level.

Up until the late 1960s, cheap, poor quality, high alcohol wines were the mainstay of the Washington wine industry. Usually made from Concord or other labrusca or hybrid grapes, the wines were often labeled port and were the classic drink of the skid road bottle-of-port-for-lunch-bunch.

Such wines have largely faded from the Washington wine scene. Now, at completely the opposite end of the spectrum, Washington has begun producing truly premium port, targeted to match the quality level of the Portuguese product.

Potassium Bitartrate

See tartrates.

Potassium Sorbate

See sorbates.

Press Juice

See press wine.

Press Wine

After crushing, some juice runs freely from the crushed grapes, but the remaining juice is yielded only after pressing, i.e., squeezing the juice out of the grapes.

White wines are fermented after pressing, and after the grape skins have been removed. Red wines are fermented with the skins and are not pressed until fermentation has finished or nearly finished. The term press *juice* usually applies to white wines since the the grapes are pressed prior to fermentation. Press *wine* usually applies to red wines, since the grape juice will have fermented into wine before pressing.

Press juice is less sweet than free run juice. Press juice and press wine are more astringent than free run juice or wine. Wine is usually made from a combination of press and free run. The last juice or wine from a very heavy pressing is very astringent and lacks fruit. Heavy press fractions are sometimes kept separately for adding to less expensive blended wines. *See free run.*

Pruning

Exceptionally vigorous plants, grape vines must be tamed and trained to produce good yields of quality fruit. The vines are cut and shaped in accordance with the chosen training and trellising system. Each year the vines are pruned severely. On a mature vine, nearly all the prior year's growth is removed. In some instances, the vines may also be pruned during the course of the growing season. *See cane training, cordon training, hedging, training, trellis.*

Pumping Over

The grape skins and pulp are left in the juice during the fermentation of red wines. This mass of skins and pulp rises to the surface and must be periodically remixed back into the fermenting juice. The technique of pumping over accomplishes this by pumping the fermenting juice back over the floating cap of skins and pulp, breaking the cap apart, and remixing it.

Pumping over, rather than punching down, the other main method of remixing the mass of skins and pulp, is well-suited to moderate to large scale production, where larger, more vertically shaped tanks are the rule for fermenting containers. Pumping over does not physically break down and macerate the mass of skins and pulp as effectively as punching down.

In the Northwest, pumping over is most widespread in Washington, where wineries are generally larger. Additionally, because of the nature of the grape and wine, Washington's major red grape varieties, Cabernet Sauvignon and Merlot, may benefit less from the physical maceration of punching down than Oregon's major red grape variety, Pinot Noir. *See cap, maceration, punching down.*

Punching Down

During the fermentation of red wines, the floating mass of skins and pulp must be remixed back into the fermenting juice. The technique of punching down accomplishes this by forcing a plunger through the floating cap of pulp and skins, breaking the cap apart and remixing it.

If the tank or container is not too large, and if the punching down is sufficiently industrious, the action also squeezes and helps macerate the pulp and skins. Advocates of punching down, with some good reason, claim that more and better flavors are extracted from the grapes than by "pumping over," the other main method of remixing the pulp and skins.

Punching down is best suited to small scale production, where fermenting containers are relatively small. Traditionally, punching down was accomplished by getting into the fermenting vat and stomping and punching by foot. The firm but soft nature of the human foot is considered the ideal implement for breaking down the pulp and skins.

In the Northwest, punching down is most widespread in Oregon, but as Oregon wineries grow larger, pumping over is being employed more frequently. *See cap, maceration, pumping over.*

Puyallup River Valley

A minor western Washington grape growing area located south and east of the city of Tacoma.

Racking

The process of separating wine from the sediment of yeast cells and pulp (lees) that settles out of the wine after fermentation. Traditionally, the wine is drawn off its sediment into clean barrels. The process is usually repeated several times until the wine is clear and little sediment remains. At that point, the wine can be bottled. *See lees.*

Rain Shadow

A climatological phenomenon involving the blockage of moist air by a vertical land mass. The rain shadow effect plays a major role in defining the Northwest's winegrowing climates.

In Oregon, the low Coast Range Mountains, running north to south along the coast, allow some marine air to flow into Oregon's interior valleys, but create enough of a rain shadow so growing conditions are not too cool or too wet—one of the few winegrowing climates ideal for the difficult but great grape, Pinot Noir.

Further inland, the towering Cascade Mountain Range runs north to south through Washington and Oregon. Its rain shadow effectively blocks moist marine air for hundreds of miles, creating a near desert, and a unique combination of conditions in Washington's Columbia Valley and Idaho's Snake River Valley that ripen grapes with intense fruit, high sugars, and crisp acidity.

Rattlesnake Hills

The northern boundary of Washington's Yakima Valley. Created when the northern movement of coastal land masses buckled the western part of the Columbia Valley, the Rattlesnake Hills form an east-west ridge that helps protect the Yakima Valley from winter Arctic air. Most of the Yakima Valley's vineyards are located on the sunny, south facing, lower slopes of the Rattlesnake Hills.

Red Hills of Dundee

See Dundee Hills.

Red Mountain

At the far eastern end of Washington's Yakima Valley, the Yakima River runs into Red Mountain and makes a radical turn northward before hooking back to merge with the Columbia River. Red Mountain is really more of a treeless hill than a mountain, but its lower slopes offer one of the warmest and best grape growing sites in the Yakima Valley.

Red Mountain is emerging as one of Washington's prime grape growing areas. Its vineyards produce excellent Cabernet Sauvignon, showing a more textural, less weedy character than other parts of the Yakima Valley. Located outside the land encompassed by the irrigation canal systems, Red Mountain was not developed until the mid 1970s, when the partners in Kiona Vineyards drilled a successful irrigation well.

Regions I-V

A classification of winegrowing climates formulated at the University of California at Davis. Climates are classified into regions by the summation of heat received during the growing season. Region I is the coolest climate, region V the warmest. This system may be the best guide for determining where wine grapes can be grown, but it is nevertheless a rather crude measure. Outside of California, particularly in the Northwest, the system tells relatively little about where to grow which grapes to make the finest wine. *See heat units.*

Residual Sugar

Wine that still has unfermented grape sugar is said to have residual sugar. The typical slightly sweet Riesling is an example of a wine with residual sugar. Residual sweetness is an alternate term. *See sweet.*

Riddling

After bottle fermented sparkling wines have completed their secondary fermentation, a residue of yeast sediment remains. The first step in eliminating the sediment is called riddling. The bottles are placed in racks at a moderate upside down angle. The bottles are rotated and bumped, gradually turning them upside down. At this point, the sediment of yeast will have settled to the base of the cork, ready to be disgorged. Except for special and expensive riddling machines suited to large scale operations, the process is all completed by hand. *See bottle fermented, disgorging, secondary fermentation.*

Ripeness

Ripeness, and the sugar content of grapes are not equatable. Grapes grown in cool climates get physiologically ripe at lower sugar levels than grapes grown in warmer climates. Physiological ripeness, not sugar content, determines the character and flavor of the grapes—and ultimately, the wine.

Specific physiological changes in the grape take place during the growing season, including maturation of the pips (grape seeds) and veraison (coloration of the grapes). In the cooler grape growing climates of Europe and western Oregon, these changes take place at lower sugar levels. (The major grape growing areas of Washington and Idaho generally fall into this categorization as well, but their climates are unique, and several other factors play a role.)

Conversely, in warmer growing climates such as southern Europe and parts of California, ripenness does not occur until grapes have reached high sugar levels. This can result in overly alcoholic, hot tasting wines. Furthermore, ripening in warmer climates typically takes place under intense heat, diminishing natural grape acids and flavor constituents.

Rootstock

Because the dreaded phylloxera root louse attacks and destroys *Vitis vinifera* grape vines, the grape species responsible for the great wines of the world, nearly all European and California grape vines are grafted onto the more resistant native American rootstocks.

In the Northwest, almost no grape vines are grafted. The soil, isolation from other vines, and absence of the phylloxera louse have prevented the spread of phylloxera. Eventually, some vines may need to be grafted, but Washington's dry sandy soil is a continuing deterrent.

Royal Slope

A gently sloping extension of the Frenchman Hills, the Royal Slope is among the more northerly winegrowing areas in Washington's Columbia Valley. Few vineyards are planted, and there is only minimal experience with the area.

Roza Canal

One of two main irrigation canals in the Yakima Valley. The Roza Canal is more northerly and at a slightly higher elevation than the Sunnyside Canal. Together, these two irrigation canals make the Yakima Valley's intense agricultural development possible. Most vineyards in the Yakima Valley get their irrigation water from one of these two canals.

Saddle Mountains

One of the east-west ridges created when the northern movement of coastal land masses buckled the western part of the Columbia Valley. *See Wahluke Slope.*

Sagemoor Farms

Washington state's largest, independent, wine grape growing enterprise. Situated along the Columbia River near the Tri-Cities, Sagemoor Farms was one of the principal grape suppliers to new wineries in the early years of Washington's modern wine industry.

Secondary Fermentation

Champagne and other sparkling wines get their sparkle from a secondary fermentation. After the base wine has finished fermenting, a measured mixture of yeast and sugar is added, and the wine is kept sealed so that the carbon dioxide, a by-product of fermentation, is trapped in the wine.

The secondary fermentation can take place in individual bottles or in a large tank (or a combination of the two methods). Bottle fermented sparkling wines are generally regarded as superior. *See bottle fermented, Charmat process.*

Set

See berry set.

Shot Berries

Poor conditions during bloom or poor nutrition may prevent the grape flowers from setting a full cluster of healthy grapes. Some of the grape berries may fail to form at all, or may form tiny, seedless, imperfect grapes known as shot berries. A cluster may contain fully-formed, healthy berries interspersed with imperfect, shot berries. *See bloom, berry set.*

Skin Contact

Red wines are fermented on the skins to extract the color and tannin. Grape skins are removed before fermenting white wines, but, depending on the grape variety, the flavors desired, and the winemaker's preferences, the skins may be allowed to macerate in the juice for a period of hours before pressing and fermentation begin.

Skookumchuck Valley

Located in western Washington, southeast of the state capitol of Olympia, the Skookumchuck Valley is site of a very small scale wine grape growing enterprise.

Slope

In premium grape growing regions, the slope of the land is critical in selecting a vineyard site. In hot growing climates, slope has relatively little importance, and grapes are routinely planted on easily farmed flat land. Cool climate grape growing is another matter.

Sloped land allows air movement and air drainage. Cold air flows downhill, away from the vines, and warm air rises to warm them. This protects the vines from frost, allows them to get an earlier start on the day, and extends the growing season in spring and fall. Secondly, premium, cool climate winegrowing regions are located further from the equator. Sloped vineyards more closely match the angle of the sun during the growing season, so that each vine gets the most sun exposure.

The Columbia Valley, Washington's major winegrowing area, is relatively flat. Few vineyards are on pronounced slopes, but some degree of slope is critical to allow air drainage and to protect the vines from damaging frosts and winter freezes. Catching the absolute maximum rays of sunlight is less critical than in Oregon's cooler, more temperate, Willamette Valley, where frosts are a minor concern, but maximum sun exposure on more steeply sloped vineyards is a priority.

Snake River Valley

Idaho's major winegrowing region. The Snake River Valley cuts a broad crescent through southern Idaho. The eastern half of the valley is a very broad, flat, nearly featureless lava plain. Toward the west, the valley narrows, and the landscape is featured with lakebeds, terraces, small canyons, and open valleys created by the Boise River and other streams that feed into the Snake. Nearly all of Idaho's vineyards are situated on south facing slopes at the western end of the Snake River Valley.

The climate is similar to Washington's Columbia Valley, but Idaho's vineyards are further inland, and planted above the 2,000 foot level. The Snake River Valley's growing season is typically shorter and more intense than the Columbia Valley's growing season. Frosts and winter cold are a threat to the vines in some years, but careful viticultural practices minimize the impact.

Riesling and Chardonnay are the most successful and widely planted grape varieties. Red wine grapes have not yet shown great promise, but other white wine grapes such as Gewurztraminer and Chenin Blanc produce quality wine.

Soil

Europeans tend to regard soil as a major factor in wine character and quality. New World winemakers, particularly those with formal training in schools such as U. C. Davis, tend to think of soil type as a minor factor as long as the basics such as adequate drainage and soil pH are in line with the vine's needs for healthy and fruitful growth.

The importance of soil probably falls somewhere in the middle ground of the two disparate views. Where the climate is more marginal for the grape variety grown (which is to say in the world's finest grape growing regions) soil characteristics seem to play more of a role.

The soils in the Columbia Valley, Washington's major grape growing area, are sandy, silty, and loamy. They are seldom clay-like, and, contrary to popular belief, they are not volcanic. The volcanic contributions such as the recent Mount St. Helens eruption are a negligible part of the soil. The soils typically contain calcium carbonate and are neutral to slightly basic.

The soils of Oregon's major grape growing areas in the western part of the state are more variable. They are generally more clay-like and slightly acidic. Some are sedimentary, others are volcanic in origin. Well drained clay loams on hillside sites are the most common vineyard soils.

Sorbates

A chemical additive, generally in the form of potassium sorbate, to prevent a wine with residual sweetness from starting fermentation again. Unfortunately, the amount of sorbate needed to prevent fermentation also contributes off flavors variously described as cotton candy or talcum powder. Sorbates mask the clarion message of the wine's varietal fruit. Resorting to sorbates is simply poor winemaking.

In the earlier days of the Northwest wine industry, many Rieslings produced by smaller wineries with fewer technical resources were cursed with sorbates. Ironically, so typical was the sorbate taste, it was sometimes mistaken for Northwest Riesling character. Northwest winemaking technique has improved greatly, even among the newest and smallest wineries, and few Northwest wines taste of sorbates.

Southwest Washington

Most of western Washington is cool and rainy, and suited only to the coolest climate grape varieties. The winegrowing climate in the southwest corner of Washington, however, differs from the rest of western Washington. Jutting southward behind the northern reaches of Oregon's coastal mountains, the climate of southwest Washington is warmer and drier, and more similar to Oregon's northern Willamette Valley. It is one of the few, if not the only, Washington winegrowing area suited to Pinot Noir.

Sparkling Wine

Wine with entrapped carbon dioxide. Upon opening, the gas is released as bubbles. Champagne is a common synonym for sparkling wine, but, more properly, Champagne is a sparkling wine from the Champagne district in France.

All the Northwest states, Oregon, Washington, Idaho, and Montana, produce sparkling wine. Oregon is particularly notable in that it is a prime region for Pinot Noir as well as Chardonnay, the two classic grapes of Champagne. In the Northwest states, and particularly in Oregon, grape ripeness is achieved at lower sugar levels, a must for the highest quality sparkling wine.

Northwest sparkling wines are almost always bottle fermented. Idaho also produces sparkling wines by the the Charmat process. *See bottle fermented, Charmat process.*

Spacing

See vine spacing.

Spritz

Originally Spritzig (or the alternate French term, petillant) referred to wine that was bottled before fermentation was complete. As the wine finished fermentation in the bottle, the carbon dioxide by-product became trapped in the wine. When the wine was later opened and poured, the carbon dioxide was released as bubbles. Unlike Champagne and other similar sparkling wines, spritzig wines are only slightly sparkling.

Now, more commonly, spritz refers to bubbles present in a non-Champagne style wine for any reason. A wine may also be "spritzy" for other reasons, such as a malolactic fermentation that starts or continues after the wine is bottled, or a wine that is fermented and bottled at cool temperatures without the opportunity for the dissolved carbon dioxide to be released.

Some Northwest winemakers purposely bottle wine, typically Riesling and Chenin Blanc, with trapped carbon dioxide to give the wine a refreshing liveliness. Dissolved carbon dioxide in red wines is an annoyance, but not a critical concern.

A malolactic fermentation that continues in the bottle produces undesirable flavors and unbalances the wine. It is a significant flaw (except for a few unusual wine types made in other parts of the world).

In red wines, spritz that persists over time and does not dissipate is a bad omen, usually indicating an unfinished yeast or malolactic fermentation. Such wines inevitably get worse with age.

Spur Pruning

The canes (vine shoots) from the preceding year's growth are pruned back to short spurs. Each spur holds several buds which will become the new growth canes for the coming year. This is the pruning method used for cordon trained vines. Cordon training and spur pruning are the predominant methods in Washington and Idaho. *See pruning, cordon training, training.*

Stemmer-Crusher

A piece of equipment used to crush the grapes and separate them from their stems and stalks prior to fermentation.

Stemmy

A green, astringent taste that can come from leaving the stems in with the crushed grapes during fermentation. *See stems.*

Stems

In modern winemaking, the grape stems are usually separated from the grapes as the grapes are crushed. Sometimes, winemakers may decide to leave all or a portion of the stems in the juice during fermentation. This practice is most often employed with Pinot Noir. In the Northwest, Oregon works most with stems. Some Oregon winemakers routinely ferment their Pinot Noir with stems, but many do not.

Stems, in a sense, ripen as do grapes. Green stems impart a harsh stemminess to a wine. Brown stems can contribute positive structure and flavor elements. Stems tend to ripen better in warm years, just the sort of vintages that can benefit from their tannins and structural elements.

Stretch Island

In the late 1800s, Adam Eckert came to Stretch Island, in Washington's Puget Sound, and established a fruit and grape nursery. Eckert developed a grape he called Island Belle, a local variant of the native American variety, Campbell Early. Stretch Island subsequently faded into viticultural oblivion, but in the late 1970s, the original vineyard was revitalized.

Sulfur Dioxide

A compound used in the winemaking process, sulfur dioxide protects wine from oxidation, growth of undesirable organisms, and formation of off odors and flavors. Excess sulfur dioxide in a finished wine, however, is an off odor itself. It can cause a tickling or stinging sensation in the nose, and may bring on sneezing. This effect is most apparent in young white wines. Vigorously swirling the wine in the glass will take care of most of the problem.

Sunnyside Canal

The Sunnyside and Roza Canals bring irrigation water from the Yakima River to the valley's prime agricultural land. Most Yakima Valley vineyards get their irrigation water from one of these two canals.

Sun Scalding

Winter cold can threaten grape vines in the major grape growing regions of Washington and Idaho. Snow cover helps insulate vine roots from freezing, but offers its own threat as well. Bright sun, reflecting off the snow, can warm the vine greatly during daylight hours, followed by a chilling temperature drop at nightfall.

Called sun scalding, this damaging effect is more of a threat in Idaho than Washington. Idaho's weather, dominated by a winter high pressure cell, offers more extremes of snow, bright sunny days, and cold nights.

Sweet

Sugar tastes sweet. Other factors also contribute to the perception of sweetness. High alcohol, low acidity, and a warmer wine temperature contribute to a sensation of sweetness. The opposite conditions decrease perceived sweetness.

Sugar, nevertheless, is the fundamental component in the perception of sweetness. Unfermented sugar makes wine taste sweet. Most of the world's great sweet wines are made from grapes shriveled and concentrated in sugar and extract by the noble mold *Botrytis cinerea*. Others are made from grapes pressed while still frozen, called ice wines. Still others are made from exceptionally ripe grapes, high in sugar, or, in the case of port, by stopping fermentation very early, then fortifying with brandy to the desired alcohol level.

In the Northwest, sweet wines are made in Washington, Idaho, and Oregon. Washington makes sweet wines by all the principal methods, and is a major producer of botrytised sweet wines. *See Botrytis cinerea, ice wine, port.*

Sweet Reserve

Unfermented or partially fermented grape juice added to table wine or aperitif wine as a sweetener. The addition of sweet reserve is a common German winemaking technique that is also often used in America for making Riesling, or any kind of slightly sweet white wine.

A portion of unfermented grape juice is held aside. The rest of the juice is completed fermented to dryness, filtered or otherwise treated so the wine will not referment, then the sweet reserve is added to make a slightly sweet, fruity wine.

As an alternative method to sweet reserve, and one often employed where more technical control is available, all the wine is fermented. When the desired level of sweetness is reached, fermentation is halted, usually by chilling, and the wine is filtered to remove the yeast cells, then sterile bottled.

Tank

Wine tanks are made from a wide variety of materials, including wood, stainless steel, plastic, fiberglass, and concrete. In the Northwest, as well as most of the modern winemaking world, stainless steel tanks are, by far, the most common.

Stainless steel tanks are made in a variety of configurations. Red wines are sometimes fermented in low-sided, open-top tanks. White wines are typically fermented in enclosed, vertical, "jacketed" tanks. Coolant is run through the broad band or jacket around the circumference of the tank, regulating the fermentation temperature. Larger tanks are used to blend wines prior to bottling.

Tank Fermented

Most wines are "tank fermented," but some white wines, typically French Burgundies and many American Chardonnays, are fermented in small barrels. In the context of sparkling wines, the phrase has a more specialized meaning. *See Charmat process.*

Tannin

A component in wine. Tannins come from grape skins, seeds, stems, and from aging wine in wood. Tannins are astringent (puckery in the mouth) and sometimes bitter. Although these properties may seem undesirable, tannins, in the right balance, are an important element in quality wine.

White wines have relatively little tannin. In a fruity white wine, such as the typical Riesling, tannin detracts from the perception of fruitiness and freshness, and bitter elements seem more pronounced. Moderate tannin is an integral part of other white wines, such as the typical oak aged Chardonnay, contributing structure and helping longevity. But even here, very much tannin makes the wine taste harsh.

Tannin is a far more major element in red wines. Tannin protects wine and helps it age. Young red wines are often quite tannic. As wine ages, the tannins combine with other compounds and drop out as sediment. Ideally, the maturation of flavors matches the decrease in tannins so that all elements of the wine are in balance.

The astringency of tannins refreshes the palate and compliments food, and tannins help wine age. In excess, however, tannins are unpleasant, and they are no magic solution to wine longevity. In the late 1970s, premium American red wines were frequently made in a high alcohol, very high tannin, low acid style. It was thought that they would be long-lived, great wines. They were neither. No amount of tannin can help wines that are short on fruit, acidity, and balance.

Pinot Noir usually has moderate tannins. Other red wines, such as Cabernet Sauvignon, are typically quite tannic. Tannic astringency in young red wines is an expected and desirable element—but only if the other components are in balance.

Tartaric Acid

The major acid in grapes, and the strongest of the grape acids. Tartaric acid, through its important role in determining wine pH, has a major effect on the taste, color, biological stability, and aging ability of wine. *See pH, acidity, and total acidity.*

Tartrates

Tartaric acid and potassium in grape juice combine to form potassium bitartrate. Potassium bitartrate is marginally soluble. If wine is cellared for a lengthy period, or chilled, the potassium bitartrate will drop out of the wine in the form of tartrate crystals.

Harmless and tasteless, the crystals are the same substance as the cooking item cream of tartar.

Because consumers sometimes think the crystals are glass chips, many winemakers cold stabilize their wines (especially white wine) by lowering the temperature below 32 degrees to precipitate the tartrates. Tartrate precipitation slightly changes the acid and pH balance of wine, and some winemakers cold stabilize for this reason as well.

Tectonic Plates

The earth's crust is composed of about a dozen moving plates, traveling in different directions, and at different rates. In the Northwest, the oceanic plate has been colliding with the continental plate for many millions of years, a process that continues today, as evidenced by geologic events such as the massive volcanic eruption of Mount St. Helens on May 18, 1980. The collision of tectonic plates is largely responsible for the dramatic geologic features that shape America's Northwest winegrowing climate.

The Coast Range in Oregon shelters the state's winegrowing regions from cool, wet, marine air, and makes premium wine possible. This geologic jumble of mountains was formed as the oceanic plate slipped beneath the continental plate, uplifting the continental plate, and scraping off some of the oceanic plate along the way. Oregon's famed Willamette Valley was itself uplifted from the sea by this process.

The oceanic plate heated and became molten as it sunk beneath the continental plate. A hundred miles inland, the molten oceanic plate resurfaced to form the Cascade Mountain Range, a towering wall of volcanic mountains running north to south through Washington and Oregon. What was once the ocean floor, now caps the continent with majestic peaks. The Cascades, far higher than the Coast

Range, almost totally block the flow of marine air for hundreds of miles inland, creating one of the world's most unique winegrowing climates, Washington's vast, arid Columbia Valley.

Thief

A pipette used for withdrawing samples of wine from a barrel. Usually made of glass in the shape of a kitchen bulb baster. At the top, instead of a bulb, is a finger handle, and an open top for the thumb. The thief is inserted into the bung hole of a barrel, the thumb placed over the top opening, the thief withdrawn and placed into a wine glass (or other sampling vessel), and the thumb removed from the top opening until the desired amount of wine is released.

Titratable Acidity

See total acidity.

Topping

Wine kept in wood barrels evaporates, creating an air space. The air space threatens wine with oxidation, volatile acidity, and other contamination. Careful cellaring practices call for frequent "topping up" or "topping off." In this procedure, wine of the same kind, often kept in one to five gallon glass containers, is poured into the cask to top it off, eliminating any air space. *See ullage.*

Total Acidity

Sometimes also termed titratable acidity, total acidity is one of the ways of measuring the acidity of a solution. Total acidity is measured by neutralizing the acids with a base of known concentration. Total acidity is typically expressed as grams of acid per 100 milliliters, or as grams of acid per liter. The different acids in wine vary in strength. In America, total acidity is expressed as if all the acids were tartaric. In France, sulfuric acid is the standard of measure. *See acidity and pH.*

Trellis

The support system for the grape vines. Sometimes consisting of a single stake for each vine, but more often a system of posts and wire strung out in long rows. *See training.*

Training

Left alone, grape vines grow wildly and vigorously, and produce very little fruit. The practice of training the vines to get more grapes has evolved into a complex science, craft, and art. Seemingly countless training system variations have emerged to address any number of winegrowing issues.

Some of the factors affected by vine training systems include crop size, grape ripeness, sugar content of the grapes, acidity, pH, taste of the fruit and wine, winter hardiness, frost resistance, crop yield, berry set, consistency of crop size, labor skill and expense, machinery type and expense, insect and disease resistance, and on and on. All training systems are a compromise. The grape growing climate, a multifaceted concern in itself, is the single most important factor in deciding on a training method.

In the Northwest, vine training is based on two basic systems, cordon training, and cane training. Bilateral cordon training is the principal training system in Washington and Idaho. In Oregon, most winegrowers rely on arc-cane training. *See cane training, canopy management, cordon training, Geneva Double Curtain, pruning.*

Ullage

The air space between the top of a wine container and the wine. Ullage in barrels threatens wine with oxidation, volatile acidity, and other contamination. Older bottles of wine may become excessively ullaged. If the air space extends below the neck of the bottle, the wine's health is in jeopardy, and the wine should be consumed (in most instances) without delay, before its condition deteriorates further. *See topping.*

Umpqua Valley

One of Oregon's oldest grape growing regions, dating back to the 1800s, the Umpqua Valley remained largely dormant in the 1900s, until the early 1960s, when Hillcrest's Richard Sommer established a vineyard near Roseburg. Sommer's vineyard marked the rebirth of Oregon's winegrowing industry and its modern day renaissance.

In April of 1984, the BATF formally recognized the Umpqua Valley as a designated viticultural area. Located in western Oregon, south of the Willamette Valley, the Umpqua Valley covers approximately 1,200 square miles. The valley is not an open basin, but an interconnected series of many small mountains, hillsides, and river drainages. The more restricted nature of the area lends itself to small or moderate size vineyards and wineries.

The Umpqua Valley is warmer and drier than the Willamette Valley to the north, and its growing season is slightly shorter. Many grape varieties are grown in the Umpqua, from Riesling and Pinot Noir to Cabernet Sauvignon and even Zinfandel. The choice of variety is dependent as much on the individual growing site and the preference of the wine-grower as on any definitive climatic imperative.

Upland Winery

Washington's first vinifera grape winery, founded by William B. Bridgman shortly after Repeal of Prohibition. Vinifera wine grapes had been sporadically planted and made into wine much earlier, but Bridgman's Yakima Valley winery in Sunny-side was the first to focus on premium vinifera wines.

The wines and consumer tastes did not mesh, and Washington's first premium vinifera winery eventually sank into oblivion. Commercial vinifera wine-making would languish in the dark ages until its renaissance in the late 1960s. *See American Wine-growers, Associated Vintners.*

Varietal

See variety.

Variety

The world's great wine grapes are all varieties of the same species, *Vitis vinifera.* The species includes both red and white wine grapes. Cabernet Sauvignon, Chardonnay, Pinot Noir, and Riesling, as examples, are all varieties of the species *Vitis vinifera.*

Veraison

A French term for a stage in the grape's maturity when the grape begins to take on color and ripen.

Vine Spacing

The density of vines in the world's vineyards ranges from a few hundred vines per acre to a few thousand vines per acre. Until recently, California's U.C. Davis researchers regarded dense vine spacing as an uneconomical, archaic practice. U.C. Davis regarded a loose vine density of around 500 vines per acre as a typical optimum for most grape varieties and growing areas.

Traditionally, cooler growing climates have had denser vine spacings. It is increasingly recognized that these traditions are more than archaic practices. Although more costly to plant and maintain, densely planted vineyards produce more consistent yields from year to year, and thus, overall, higher yields. The grapes, and therefore the wines, have a better chemical structure and more intense flavors. In cooler years, the grapes ripen more reliably. Individual vines have less of a production burden, more vertical root structures, and are better able to withstand and recover from frosts and winter freezing.

Even in the relatively warm growing climates of California, denser vine spacing is gaining favor. In the cooler Northwest, denser vine spacing is all the more important. In the cool climate of western Oregon's Willamette Valley, vine densities of double to triple U.C Davis's original recommendations are routine.

Vinifera

See Vitis vinifera.

Vinification

Fermenting the grapes into wine.

Vintage

The year the grapes are grown, harvested, and made into wine. Each year, each vintage, is different. Cooler growing climates experience greater vintage variation. Washington and Idaho vintages generally vary more than California vintages. Oregon vintages, and those of most of Europe's great growing regions, vary more than Washington and Idaho vintages.

Although the wine usually bespeaks the character of the vintage, and some vintages are better than others, individual wines may be either far below or far above the overall quality of the vintage. The well-worn saw bears repeating, remembering, and practicing—Good wines are made in poor years, poor wines are made in good years. Buy wines, not vintages.

Viticultural Area

Beginning January 1, 1983, new Bureau of Alcohol Tobacco and Firearms regulations made provisions for establishing viticultural areas as appellations of origin on wine labels and in advertising. Under the regulations, a viticultural area is a delimited grape growing region or area with geographic features that distinguish it from surrounding areas. The use of a viticultural area on a wine label indicates that at least 85 percent of the wine is produced from grapes grown in that area.

Anyone can submit a petition for a viticultural area. The petition must demonstrate that the area is regionally or nationally known as referring to the area under petition, that there is current or historical evidence to that effect, and that geographic features set the area apart from surrounding areas. Viticultural areas can cross state, county, and other political boundaries.

In the Northwest, the Yakima Valley, Columbia Valley, Walla Walla Valley, Willamette Valley, and Umpqua Valley are designated viticultural areas. The Columbia Valley is the largest viticultural area, encompassing the Yakima Valley and Walla Walla Valley viticultural areas, and crossing state boundaries, including land in Washington and Oregon.

Viticulture

Grape growing.

Vitis Labrusca

A native American grape species. Concord is the best known variety of the species. Its strong flavor is typified by the ubiquitous grape jelly and juice drinks. The flavor works relatively well in the classic schoolchild cuisine, the peanut butter-and-jelly-sandwich, but it is entirely unsuited to quality wine. Except as unusual oddities, *Vitis labrusca* grapes play no role in the Northwest wine industry.

Vitis Vinifera

The species of grape responsible for all the world's greatest wines. The Northwest's grape wine industry is based almost entirely on *Vitis vinifera* grapes. The famous French Bordeaux and Burgundy wines are made from vinifera grapes. Cabernet Sauvignon, Chardonnay, Pinot Noir, and Riesling are examples of vinifera varieties.

Except for California and a few, hot, Southwest growing climates, the Northwest is the only major American winegrowing region based on premium vinifera grape wines. Most other regions rely heavily on varieties of native American species such as *Vitis labrusca* and *Vitis riparia*, or on French-American hybrids.

Wadenswil

A clone of Pinot Noir. Of the two most widely planted Oregon Pinot Noir clones, Wadenswil is reputed to be slightly less colored and intense, but more highly scented, with complex, delicate flavors. This distinction has some merit, but the vineyard site, grape growing practices, and winemaking style have a far greater effect on the wine than clonal distinctions. Oregon's oldest Willamette Valley Pinot Noir vineyard, David Lett's Eyrie Vineyard, is principally the Wadenswil clone. *See clone, Pommard, Gamay.*

Wahluke Slope

One of the newer and more promising grape growing areas in Washington's Columbia Valley, the Wahluke Slope is among the valley's warmest and most protected grape growing sites. Located on the gently sloping, lower, southern reaches of the Saddle Mountains, the south facing Wahluke Slope is well sheltered from the cold arctic air.

Walla Walla Valley

In March of 1984, the BATF formally recognized the Walla Walla Valley viticultural area. Part of the more encompassing Columbia Valley appellation, the Walla Walla Valley, like the Columbia Valley, includes land in both Washington and Oregon. Also like the Columbia Valley, most of Walla Walla Valley winegrowing and winemaking is centered on the Washington side of the border, in the southeastern part of the state.

A small viticultural area, the Walla Walla Valley encompasses 280 square miles. The climate is varied, but it is generally slightly more moist and temperate than most of the Columbia Valley. Walla Walla Valley Cabernet Sauvignon shows particular promise.

Washington

Washington produces more premium *Vitis vinifera* wine grapes than any other state in America, except California. Wine grapes have been grown in Washington since the 1800s. After a period of little activity, the end of Prohibition saw a flurry of new wineries.

The focus, regrettably, was on cheap, low quality wines made primarily from labrusca grapes. Washington winegrowing sank into a long decline. The rebirth of the Washington wine industry, based solely on premium *Vitis vinifera* grape varieties, did not come until the late 1960s.

Today, Washington has 11,000 acres of premium vinifera wine grapes. Nearly all of Washington's grapes are grown east of the Cascade Mountain Range in the vast Columbia Valley. The Columbia Valley includes the Yakima and Walla Walla Valleys within its boundaries. Other grape growing areas include the Columbia Gorge, the Puget Sound area, and Southwest Washington.

Riesling is by far the most widely planted grape, but its percentage is declining as increasing attention is devoted to Chardonnay, Semillon, Sauvignon Blanc, Cabernet Sauvignon, Merlot, Chenin Blanc, and other grape varieties. Washington's red wines, once overshadowed by the predominance of Riesling, are among Washington's finest wines.

Willamette Valley

By far Oregon's biggest winegrowing region, in size, vineyard acreage, and number of wineries, the Willamette Valley was formally recognized as a viticultural area by the BATF in January of 1984.

The Willamette Valley covers 5,200 square miles of western Oregon landscape. Forming an elongated "V" narrowing to the south, the Willamette Valley runs from Oregon's northern border, on the Columbia River, south to the city of Eugene, half way down the state. Most of the vineyards and wineries are located on sloping hillsides along the western edge of the valley.

The Willamette Valley's western boundary, the Coast Range mountains, partially blocks the on-shore flow of Pacific marine air and prevents the climate from being too cool and rainy. Enough marine effect remains, however, so that the Willamette Valley is ideally suited to cool climate grape varieties such as Pinot Noir and Chardonnay. The Willamette Valley is one of the very few places in the world where that most difficult but most rewarding of grapes, Pinot Noir, produces outstanding wine.

Yakima Valley

In May of 1983, Washington's Yakima Valley received the Northwest's first BATF viticultural area designation. Wholly contained within the more encompassing Columbia Valley appellation, the Yakima Valley is the most intensely developed agricultural region in the Columbia Valley.

The Yakima Valley covers slightly more than 1,000 square miles, but most of the vineyards are located on the north side of the river, along the lower slopes of the Rattlesnake Hills. It is the most geographically distinct of the Columbia Valley's major

154

grape growing areas. The Yakima Valley is shaped not so much by the river itself, but by ridges formed from basaltic uplifts in the terrain millions of years ago. Running in a generally east to west direction, the ridges define the shape of the valley.

Most of the valley is slightly cooler than other major Columbia Valley grape growing regions, but individual sites can range from quite cool to very warm. Frosts and winter cold are problems in some years. Parts of the valley are sometimes hit hard by spring or fall frosts. A wide range of grape varieties perform well in the valley. The cooler sites are excellent for Riesling, warmer sites for Cabernet Sauvignon.

Yeast

The organism responsible for turning grapes into wine. Yeast ferments grape juice, converting sugar into alcohol and carbon dioxide. The fermentation process is also responsible for many of the complex flavors and fragrances that contribute to the character of wine.

Saccharomyces cereviseae is the major yeast species used in winemaking. In European vineyards, wine yeasts are amply present in the vineyards and on the grapes. Because of this, European winemakers typically ferment the wine without a separate yeast inoculation. In the much younger American vineyards, the correct yeasts are seldom present in adequate quantity, and the grape juice is inoculated with selected yeast strains. In the Northwest and elsewhere in the new world, attempts at fermenting the juice with wild yeasts more often than not result in off flavors and stuck fermentations.

Many strains of *Saccharomyces cereviseae* have been developed to serve different fermentation needs. Delicate, fruity, white wines require strains that can ferment reliably at low temperatures. Rich Chardonnays benefit from yeast strains that ferment vigorously and produce round, full flavors.

In some instances, entirely different yeast species are chosen. The sweet French Sauternes, for example, are fermented with *Saccharomyces bailli*, a yeast that ferments fructose sugar faster than glucose sugar. When the fermentation is stopped, a higher ratio of the less sweet tasting glucose remains, and the wine is rich and sweet without being cloyingly so.

Yield

Yield usually refers to tons of grapes per acre. Yield may also refer to number of gallons of wine per ton of grapes.

Yield from a vineyard varies greatly according to the growing site and climatic conditions, the grape variety, and the viticultural practices of the grape grower. Washington vineyards inherently produce higher yields of grapes with good sugar and acid balance than do Oregon vineyards. Some varieties, such as Pinot Noir, yield fewer tons of grapes than other varieties, such as Chenin Blanc. Three tons an acre is a typical yield for Oregon Pinot Noir, versus 10 or more tons an acre for Washington Chenin Blanc.

By pruning and cluster thinning, a grower can adjust the yield. Although a continuing subject of debate, it is generally agreed that lower yields produce the best grapes. Some grapes, such as Pinot Noir, are particularly sensitive to yield. Three or fewer tons per acre is desirable for the best Pinot Noir.

In Washington, high yields can overstress the vine, allowing it less time and energy reserves to prepare itself for winter. Twelve tons an acre may produce reasonably good Chenin Blanc, but if the winter is harsh, this winter sensitive variety can suffer damage and a greatly reduced crop in subsequent years.

Yield may also refer to to the amount of wine produced from each ton of grapes. A ton of grapes yields approximately 130 to 180 gallons of wine. The yield varies according to winery equipment and winemaking practices. Sophisticated wine presses and centrifuge equipment yield more wine per ton. Heavier pressing yields more wine, but the final portion is less fruity, more bitter, and more astringent, diminishing the quality of the wine.

O r d e r   F o r m

❧   ❧   ❧   ❧   ❧

Also by Ted Jordan Meredith—

The Wines and Wineries of America's Northwest

The New York Times calls this book *"...thorough and informative...first rate."*

A comprehensive look at the wines, wineries, and winegrowing regions of Oregon, Washington, and Idaho. This book has become the authoritative reference on America's second largest premium wine-growing region.

❧   ❧   ❧   ❧   ❧

Please send me the following books—

_____ copies of **The Wines and Wineries of America's Northwest** at $12.95 each.

_____ copies of **Northwest Wine Companion** at $8.95 each.

I am enclosing a total of _____ which includes $1.00 for the first book and $.50 for each additional book (Washington residents also add 8.1% sales tax.).

❑ I have the books I need now, but please add me to your mailing list to receive early notice of your newest wine books.

Name _____

Address _____

City_____ State____ Zip _____

Nexus Press, P.O. Box 911, Kirkland, WA 98083

O r d e r   F o r m

❦   ❦   ❦   ❦   ❦

Also by Ted Jordan Meredith—

The Wines and Wineries of America's Northwest

The New York Times calls this book *"...thorough and informative...first rate."*

A comprehensive look at the wines, wineries, and winegrowing regions of Oregon, Washington, and Idaho. This book has become the authoritative reference on America's second largest premium winegrowing region.

❦   ❦   ❦   ❦   ❦

Please send me the following books—

_____ copies of **The Wines and Wineries of America's Northwest** at $12.95 each.

_____ copies of **Northwest Wine Companion** at $8.95 each.

I am enclosing a total of _____which includes $1.00 for the first book and $.50 for each additional book (Washington residents also add 8.1% sales tax.).

❏ I have the books I need now, but please add me to your mailing list to receive early notice of your newest wine books.

Name_____

Address_____

City_____State____ Zip_____

Nexus Press, P.O. Box 911, Kirkland, WA 98083